OPPOSING VIEWPOINTS® SERIES

The Wealth Gap

Other Books of Related Interest

Opposing Viewpoints Series

Bankruptcy
The Middle Class
The Minimum Wage
Tax Reform

At Issue Series

Are Executives Paid Too Much?
Corporate Corruption
Is the American Dream a Myth?
Should the Rich Pay Higher Taxes?

Current Controversies Series

Capitalism
Jobs in America
Poverty and Homelessness
The U.S. Economy

"Congress shall make no law … abridging the freedom of speech, or of the press."

First Amendment to the Constitution

The basic foundation of our democracy is the First Amendment guarantee of freedom of expression. The Opposing Viewpoints series is dedicated to the concept of this basic freedom and the idea that it is more important to practice it than to enshrine it.

**OPPOSING
VIEWPOINTS®
SERIES**

| The Wealth Gap

Susan Henneberg, Book Editor

GREENHAVEN
PUBLISHING

Published in 2017 by Greenhaven Publishing
353 3rd Avenue, Suite 255, New York, NY 10010

First Edition

Articles in Greenhaven Publishing anthologies are often edited for length to meet page
requirements. In addition, original titles of these works are changed to clearly present
the main thesis and to explicitly indicate the author's opinion. Every effort is made to
ensure that Greenhaven Publishing accurately reflects the original intent of the authors.
Every effort has been made to trace the owners of the copyrighted material.

Cover image: Spencer Platt/Getty Images News/Getty Images

Library of Congress Cataloging-in-Publication Data

Names: Henneberg, Susan, editor.
Title: The wealth gap / edited by Susan Henneberg.
Description: New York : Greenhaven Publishing, 2017. |
Series: Opposing viewpoints | Includes index.
Identifiers: LCCN ISBN 9781534500341 (pbk.) | ISBN 9781534500242 (library bound)
Subjects: LCSH: Pay equity--United States. | Equal pay for equal work--
United States. | Discrimination in employment--United States.
Classification: LCC HD6061.2.U6 H46 2017 | DDC 331.2'1530973--dc23

Manufactured in the United States of America

Website: http://greenhavenpublishing.com

Contents

The Importance of Opposing Viewpoints   10

Introduction   13

Chapter 1: Is America's Wealth Gap a Problem?

Chapter Preface   17

1. The Middle Class Is Shrinking   19
   Richard Fry and Rakesh Kochhar

2. The Wealth Gap Reaches Record High   23
   Richard Fry and Rakesh Kochhar

3. Income Inequality Is Not the Problem   28
   Thomas A. Garrett

4. US Ranks Last in Income Inequality   35
   Salvatore Babones

5. Income Inequality Has Harmed the 99 Percent   41
   Mary E. Northridge

6. Powerful Market Shifts Are to Blame for Income Inequality   45
   OpenStax CNX

Periodical and Internet Sources Bibliography   56

Chapter 2: Is the American Dream Attainable?

Chapter Preface   58

1. The American Dream Has Ended   60
   Niall Ferguson

2. Income Inequality Perpetuates Lower Social Mobility   69
   Miles Corak

3. Downward Mobility Is the New Normal   75
   Mechele Dickerson

4. The American Dream Isn't Always a Dream   82
   Ronald A. Wirtz

5. The Middle Class Is Gone   **97**
   Edward McClelland

Periodical and Internet Sources Bibliography   **102**

Chapter 3: How Can the Wealth Gap Be Addressed?

Chapter Preface   **104**

1. Government Should Narrow the Wealth Gap   **106**
   Bernie Sanders

2. Tax the Rich to Invest in the Poor   **111**
   Gary Becker and Richard Posner

3. Higher Taxes on the Rich Won't Reduce
   Income Inequality   **115**
   Doug Mataconis

4. Redistribution Is the Answer   **120**
   David Lipton

5. A Universal Basic Income Would Change the Economy   **129**
   Scott Santens

6. Reducing the Wealth Gap Will Benefit Our Institutions   **140**
   Gerald D. Jaynes

Periodical and Internet Sources Bibliography   **146**

Chapter 4: Does America's Wealth Gap Harm Society?

Chapter Preface   **148**

1. Income Equality Is Difficult to Reverse   **150**
   Christina Pazzanese

2. A Wealth Gap Creates Political Division   **162**
   Christos Makridis

3. The Wealth Gap Dimishes Opportunity   **168**
   Lawrence Mishel

4. Inequality's Disadvantages Outweigh Its Advantages   **173**
   Nicholas Birdsong

5. Capitalism Causes a Wealth Gap   **187**
   Ann Robertson and Bill Leumer

6. America Benefits from Income Inequality   **193**
   Jennifer Larino

Periodical and Internet Sources Bibliography   **198**

For Further Discussion   **199**

Organizations to Contact   **201**

Bibliography of Books   **208**

Index   **209**

The Importance of Opposing Viewpoints

Perhaps every generation experiences a period in time in which the populace seems especially polarized, starkly divided on the important issues of the day and gravitating toward the far ends of the political spectrum and away from a consensus-facilitating middle ground. The world that today's students are growing up in and that they will soon enter into as active and engaged citizens is deeply fragmented in just this way. Issues relating to terrorism, immigration, women's rights, minority rights, race relations, health care, taxation, wealth and poverty, the environment, policing, military intervention, the proper role of government—in some ways, perennial issues that are freshly and uniquely urgent and vital with each new generation—are currently roiling the world.

If we are to foster a knowledgeable, responsible, active, and engaged citizenry among today's youth, we must provide them with the intellectual, interpretive, and critical-thinking tools and experience necessary to make sense of the world around them and of the all-important debates and arguments that inform it. After all, the outcome of these debates will in large measure determine the future course, prospects, and outcomes of the world and its peoples, particularly its youth. If they are to become successful members of society and productive and informed citizens, students need to learn how to evaluate the strengths and weaknesses of someone else's arguments, how to sift fact from opinion and fallacy, and how to test the relative merits and validity of their own opinions against the known facts and the best possible available information. The landmark series Opposing Viewpoints has been providing students with just such critical-thinking skills and exposure to the debates surrounding society's most urgent contemporary issues for many years, and it continues to serve this essential role with undiminished commitment, care, and rigor.

The key to the series's success in achieving its goal of sharpening students' critical-thinking and analytic skills resides in its title— Opposing Viewpoints. In every intriguing, compelling, and engaging volume of this series, readers are presented with the widest possible spectrum of distinct viewpoints, expert opinions, and informed argumentation and commentary, supplied by some of today's leading academics, thinkers, analysts, politicians, policy makers, economists, activists, change agents, and advocates. Every opinion and argument anthologized here is presented objectively and accorded respect. There is no editorializing in any introductory text or in the arrangement and order of the pieces. No piece is included as a "straw man," an easy ideological target for cheap point-scoring. As wide and inclusive a range of viewpoints as possible is offered, with no privileging of one particular political ideology or cultural perspective over another. It is left to each individual reader to evaluate the relative merits of each argument— as he or she sees it, and with the use of ever-growing critical-thinking skills—and grapple with his or her own assumptions, beliefs, and perspectives to determine how convincing or successful any given argument is and how the reader's own stance on the issue may be modified or altered in response to it.

This process is facilitated and supported by volume, chapter, and selection introductions that provide readers with the essential context they need to begin engaging with the spotlighted issues, with the debates surrounding them, and with their own perhaps shifting or nascent opinions on them. In addition, guided reading and discussion questions encourage readers to determine the authors' point of view and purpose, interrogate and analyze the various arguments and their rhetoric and structure, evaluate the arguments' strengths and weaknesses, test their claims against available facts and evidence, judge the validity of the reasoning, and bring into clearer, sharper focus the reader's own beliefs and conclusions and how they may differ from or align with those in the collection or those of their classmates.

Research has shown that reading comprehension skills improve dramatically when students are provided with compelling, intriguing, and relevant "discussable" texts. The subject matter of these collections could not be more compelling, intriguing, or urgently relevant to today's students and the world they are poised to inherit. The anthologized articles and the reading and discussion questions that are included with them also provide the basis for stimulating, lively, and passionate classroom debates. Students who are compelled to anticipate objections to their own argument and identify the flaws in those of an opponent read more carefully, think more critically, and steep themselves in relevant context, facts, and information more thoroughly. In short, using discussable text of the kind provided by every single volume in the Opposing Viewpoints series encourages close reading, facilitates reading comprehension, fosters research, strengthens critical thinking, and greatly enlivens and energizes classroom discussion and participation. The entire learning process is deepened, extended, and strengthened.

For all of these reasons, Opposing Viewpoints continues to be exactly the right resource at exactly the right time—when we most need to provide readers with the critical-thinking tools and skills that will not only serve them well in school but also in their careers and their daily lives as decision-making family members, community members, and citizens. This series encourages respectful engagement with and analysis of opposing viewpoints and fosters a resulting increase in the strength and rigor of one's own opinions and stances. As such, it helps make readers "future ready," and that readiness will pay rich dividends for the readers themselves, for the citizenry, for our society, and for the world at large.

Introduction

> *"The wealthy are getting wealthier. As for everyone else, no such luck."*
>
> —*Patricia Cohen, "Fueled by Recession, U.S. Wealth Gap Is Widest in Decades, Study Finds,"* The New York Times, *December 17, 2014.*

On September 17, 2011, several thousand protesters gathered in a small park in New York City's Financial District. Calling themselves the "99%," the activists brought attention to the disparities in wealth and income between the wealthiest 1 percent of the U.S. population and the rest of the country's wage earners. The Occupy Wall Street demonstrators' main concerns were economic inequality, greed and corruption in the banking industries, and the perceived influence of corporations on government.

Before the Occupy Wall Street movement, there was very little media attention paid to the income and wealth gap in the United States. The Great Recession of 2007–2009 brought more immediate economic problems to the forefront. Workers worried about job layoffs, housing foreclosures, and wage stagnation. It was only as the recession ebbed and the economy began to rebound that workers realized that the economic crisis had hit families unequally. Those at the bottom of the economic ladder were left unemployed and often homeless. Those at the top were unscathed. Some even profited.

The Occupy Wall Street protesters claimed that greed and corruption in U.S. and world financial institutions had caused the global crisis. They also claimed that there was too much corporate influence on the U.S. political process, enriching the 1 percent and impoverishing the middle and lower classes. Their focus became the increasing inequality of both income and wealth between the billionaire class and those struggling to pay their mortgages. The activists pointed out that, according to the Congressional Budget Office, the average after-tax income of the top 1 percent rose 275 percent from the years 1979 to 2007, compared to 67 percent for the top 20 percent, and just 19 percent for the lowest level of workers.

While Occupy Wall Street achieved little beyond spotlighting this important issue, the topic re-emerged during the 2016 presidential campaign. In particular, the 1 percent became the target and rallying cry for the candidacy of Vermont Democratic senator Bernie Sanders. He called income and wealth inequality the great moral issue of his time. Sanders's message resonated with millions of voters. Pointing out statistics showing a massive transfer of wealth from the middle class and the poor to the wealthiest people in the country, Sanders declared it the "Robin Hood principle in reverse" on his campaign website. In speech after speech, he talked about disproportionate gains by the top 1 percent in new income, the loss of real median income by the working class, and the rise in the child poverty rate. "There is something profoundly wrong," Sanders told his supporters, "when one family owns more wealth than the bottom 130 million Americans."

In contrast to the campaign rhetoric of Senator Sanders, Republican presidential candidate Donald Trump used his wealth as a selling point in his presidential aspirations. He attributed his large net worth to his smart business skills in real estate, though critics point out that he also inherited a fortune from his real estate magnate father. Trump's sizable number of low and middle-income supporters seemed to overlook or even admire their candidate's 1 percent status.

The Occupy Wall Street movement and the 2016 presidential campaign reflect the controversies surrounding the issue of the wealth gap in America today. There is very little consensus among experts about the seriousness of the problem. Economists and politicians debate the extent of the gap between the wealthy and the poor. Some experts argue that the huge disparity in wealth is having a major impact on the ability of average wage earners to achieve the American dream of a steady job, home ownership, and college educations for their children. On the other hand, some economists believe that wealth and income inequality accompanies stronger economic growth. They point out that while America's top 1 percent holds a greater share of our nation's wealth compared to other developed countries, our middle and lower classes enjoy a higher standard of living than those in Europe.

Because of the attention paid to the wealth gap, more Americans desire a greater understanding of the economic forces behind income inequality. Globalization, technological changes in the workplace, the declining power of unions, and immigration are all concerns that touch most Americans' lives. *Opposing Viewpoints: The Wealth Gap* addresses these issues in chapters titled "Is America's Wealth Gap a Problem?" "Is the American Dream Attainable?" "How Can the Wealth Gap Be Addressed?" and "Does America's Wealth Gap Harm Society?" readers will find insights into the causes of the wealth gap in America, its extent, and possible solutions for narrowing it.

Is America's Wealth Gap a Problem?

Chapter Preface

Americans have always put economic problems first when asked to identify the biggest issue facing the country. The 2011 Occupy Wall Street and 2016 presidential election gave wage earners a vocabulary to discuss their concerns. The media began to headline the terms "income inequality," the "1 percent," and the "wealth gap." Wage earners, still recovering from the 2007–2009 recession, became aware of the disparities between themselves and the super-rich. According to a 2015 *New York Times* survey, 65 percent of those polled said that the gap between the rich and poor in the U.S. is a problem that needs to be addressed immediately. Fifty-seven percent thought that the government should do more to reduce the gap.

Economists use several methods to measure income inequality and quantify the gap between low- and high-income households. One way of describing the spectrum of inequality is to divide the distribution of household incomes into five sections, called quintiles. To compare the levels of the wealth gap among different countries, economists often use the Gini coefficient, first defined by an Italian economist in 1912. These statistics measure the degree of concentration in the distribution of income in a country. A value of 0 represents absolute equality, where income is equally distributed across all levels of society. A value of 100 represents absolute inequality. In 2013, the World Bank calculated a value of 40.8 for the U.S., well above Sweden's 25, Canada's 32.6, and Germany's 28.2.

One result of rising inequality, say Pew Research Center researchers Richard Fry and Rakesh Kochhar, is the shrinking of the middle class. In their analyses, they find that the nation's large metropolitan areas are particularly suffering from a loss of middle-income households.

Not all economists and policy experts agree that income and wealth inequality is a problem that needs to be solved. Economists such as Thomas A. Garrett argue that income inequality is a byproduct of a healthy economy. Garrett finds that there is a great deal of fluidity in people's income as life circumstances move them up and down the income spectrum. Over half the people in the 2015 *New York Times* survey were confident of a bright outlook for their own personal finances.

| "With fewer Americans in the middle-income tier, the economic tiers above and below have grown in significance over time."

The Middle Class Is Shrinking

Richard Fry and Rakesh Kochhar

In the following viewpoint, Richard Fry and Rakesh Kochhar find that the share of adults in the middle class is shrinking in US metropolitan areas. Analyzing data from a 2014 Pew Research Center survey, the authors also find that both lower-income and upper-income households increased in most areas. The data shows that the greatest shares of middle-income adults are located in the Midwest. Fry and Kochhar are researchers at the Pew Research Center.

As you read, consider the following questions:

1. What income levels do the authors consider as middle class?
2. How has the loss of income by the middle class impacted the higher and lower income levels?
3. In which areas have middle class incomes shrunk the most?

T he American middle class is shrinking at the national level, as was documented in a previous study by Pew Research Center. Our new analysis of government data finds that the middle class is also losing ground in the vast majority of metropolitan areas in the country.

Here are six key takeaways from the new report:

1 The decline in the share of adults who are middle class nationally also proved to be a pervasive local phenomenon in the period from 2000 to 2014. Affecting communities from Boston to Seattle and from Dallas to Milwaukee, the share of adults living in middle-income households fell in 203 out of 229 U.S. metropolitan areas examined from 2000 to 2014. With fewer Americans in the middle-income tier, the economic tiers above and below have grown in significance over time. The share of adults in the lower-income tier rose in 160 areas, and the share in the upper-income tier increased in 172 areas. These trends were not mutually exclusive—the shares of adults in the lower- and upper-income tiers both increased in 108 metropolitan areas.

2 The share of adults in the upper-income tier increased more than the lower-income share in about half the metropolitan areas analyzed. Across the 229 areas, adults were more likely to climb the income ladder than to descend it in 119 areas. The areas that experienced the biggest gains in economic status from 2000 to 2014 are a diverse group, including energy-based economies such as Midland, Texas; the tourism-driven locality of Barnstable Town, Massachusetts; and the meat-packing area of Amarillo, Texas. But the lower-income share increased more in 110 areas. The areas that slipped the most in economic status include Goldsboro, North Carolina, and Springfield, Ohio. Many of these areas are more reliant than average on manufacturing, but other factors likely played a role as well.

3 Nationally, the share of adults in the middle class has fallen since 2000 and the shares in lower- and upper-income tiers have increased. Reflecting the cumulative effect of changes at the local level, the national share of American adults in middle-income households decreased from 55% in 2000 to 51% in 2014. At the same time, the share of adults in the upper-income tier increased from 17% to 20%, and the share of adults in the lower-income tier increased from 28% to 29%. (The national estimates encompass *all* American adults, not just those in the 229 metropolitan areas examined in greater detail.)

4 Households in all economic tiers experienced near-universal decreases in median incomes across U.S. metropolitan areas. Middle-income households lost ground financially in 222 of 229 metropolitan areas from 1999 to 2014. Meanwhile, those in the lower-income tier saw their median income slip in 221 areas and those in the upper-income households took a financial hit in 215 areas.

5 The 10 metropolitan areas with the greatest shares of middle-income adults are located mostly in the Midwest. Wausau, Wisconsin, led on this basis, with 67% of adults living in middle-income households in 2014. It was followed closely by Janesville-Beloit, Wisconsin (65%). On the other end of the scale across all 229 areas examined was Monroe, Louisiana, where the share of adults who were middle income stood at 42%. Middle-income adults lacked a majority in 50 metropolitan areas in 2014. Metropolitan areas with the largest upper-income shares are mostly to the northeast or on the California coast, while the 10 metropolitan areas with the biggest lower-income tiers are to the southwest, several on the border with Mexico.

6 There is notable variation in the median income of middle-class households across U.S. metropolitan

areas. The median income of middle-class households was within the $70,000 to $75,000 range in 138 out of 229 areas, but it was as high as $81,283 in Racine, Wisconsin, and as low as $64,549 in Hanford-Corcoran, California. By definition, middle-class households earned from about $42,000 to $125,000, but within this range, households in an area might cluster near the top or the bottom end.

The 229 metropolitan areas we examined, out of a total of 381 currently defined by the federal government, are the ones that are identifiable in publicly available Census Bureau datasets and for which data were available for both 2000 and 2014. They accounted for 76% of the nation's population in 2014.

We define middle-income households as those whose annual household income is two-thirds to double the national median after incomes have been adjusted for household size. In 2014, this amounted to about $42,000 to $125,000 annually for a household of three. Lower-income households have incomes less than two-thirds of the median and upper-income households have incomes that are more than double the median. Incomes in each metropolitan area are adjusted for the cost of living in the area relative to the national average cost of living.

> "While most American families remain financially stuck, upper-income families have seen their median wealth double from $318,100 in 1983 to $639,400 in 2013."

The Wealth Gap Reaches Record High

Richard Fry and Rakesh Kochhar

In the following article, Richard Fry and Rakesh Kochhar find that in 2013 the wealth gap between middle-income families and those considered high-income was the highest on record. According to the authors, since the Great Recession the wealth of higher-income families has been increasing while the wealth of middle- and lower-income families has stagnated or decreased. The authors' analysis of annual Surveys of Consumer Finances shows that the wealth of upper-income households was seven times the wealth of middle-income households. Fry and Kochhar are researchers at the Pew Research Center.

"America's wealth gap between middle-income and upper-income families is widest on record," Richard Fry and Rakesh Kochhar, Pew Research Center, December 17, 2014. Reprinted by permission.

As you read, consider the following questions:

1. How do the authors distinguish between a family's wealth and income?
2. What reasons do the authors give for the increase of the wealth gap between middle- and upper-income families?
3. What was the impact of the Great Recession on middle-income families?

The wealth gap between America's high income group and everyone else has reached record high levels since the economic recovery from the Great Recession of 2007-09, with a clear trajectory of increasing wealth for the upper-income families and no wealth growth for the middle- and lower-income families.

A new Pew Research Center analysis of wealth finds the gap between America's upper-income and middle-income families has reached its highest level on record. In 2013, the median wealth of the nation's upper-income families ($639,400) was nearly seven times the median wealth of middle-income families ($96,500), the widest wealth gap seen in 30 years when the Federal Reserve began collecting these data.

In addition, America's upper-income families have a median net worth that is nearly 70 times that of the country's lower-income families, also the widest wealth gap between these families in 30 years.

Wealth is the difference between the value of a family's assets (such as financial assets as well as home, car and businesses) and debts. It is an important dimension of household well-being because it's a measure of a family's "nest egg" and can be used to sustain consumption during emergencies (for example, job layoffs) as well as provide income during retirement. Wealth is different from household income, which measures the annual inflow of wages, interests, profits and other sources of earnings. The data have also shown a growing gap in wealth along racial and ethnic lines since the recession ended.

In our analysis, we categorized families by their household income, after we adjusted their incomes for family size. Middle-income families are families whose size-adjusted income is between two-thirds and twice the median size-adjusted income. Lower-income families have a size-adjusted household income less than two-thirds the median and upper-income families more than twice the median.

This methodology results in 46% of America's families being classified as middle income in 2013. One-third of families were lower income and 21% were upper income. For a family of three in 2013, a household income of $38,100 qualifies as middle income and $114,300 or greater qualifies as upper income.

The tabulations from the Fed's data indicate that the upper-income families have begun to regain some of the wealth they lost during the Great Recession, while middle-income families haven't seen any gains. The median wealth among upper-income families increased from $595,300 in 2010 to $639,400 in 2013 (all dollar amounts in 2013 dollars). The typical wealth of middle-income families was basically unchanged in 2013—it remained at about $96,500 over the same period.

As a result, the estimated wealth gap between upper-income and middle-income families has *increased* during the recovery. In 2010, the median wealth of upper-income families was 6.2 times the median wealth of middle-income families. By 2013, that wealth ratio grew to 6.6.

To be sure, the wealth gap between upper-income and middle-income families also widened during the Great Recession. The median wealth of all three income groups declined from 2007 to 2010. But upper-income families were not hit nearly as hard as lower- and middle-income families. Median wealth declined by 17% from 2007 ($718,000) to 2010 ($595,300) among upper-income families. In contrast, middle-income (-39%) and lower-income (-41%) families had larger declines in wealth. The larger losses among middle-income families resulted in the wealth gap

SHARP PARTISAN DIVISIONS ON CAUSES OF INCOME INEQUALITY

Fully 59% of Democrats voice the view that inequality is a major national economic challenge, as do 49% of independents. But only 19% of Republicans agree.

There is also partisan disagreement on the most important reasons for the gap between the rich and the poor. Republicans (39%) are most likely to say it exists because some people work harder than others. Democrats (17%) and independents (23%) are much less likely to blame the poor's work ethic.

Republicans (28%) also say inequality is a product of government economic policies, a view held by 24% of Americans overall. Democrats (20%) and independents (25%) are less likely to point the finger at government, putting more emphasis on shortcomings of the U.S. education system. A fifth of Democrats and 17% of independents (17%) cite the educational system as the most important reason for the rich-poor gap compared with just 9% of Republicans.

"Debate over inequality highlights sharp partisan divisions on the issue," Bruce Stokes, Pew Research Center, October 20, 2014.

between upper- and middle-income families rising from 2007 (4.5) to 2010 (6.2).

The latest data reinforce the larger story of America's middle class household wealth stagnation over the past three decades. The Great Recession destroyed a significant amount of middle-income and lower-income families' wealth, and the economic "recovery" has yet to be felt for them. Without any palpable increase in their wealth since 2010, middle- and lower-income families' wealth levels in 2013 are comparable to where they were in the early 1990s.

It could help explain why, by other measures, the majority of Americans are not feeling the impact of the economic recovery, despite an improvement in the unemployment rate, stock market and housing prices. In October, just one-in-five Americans rated the country's economic conditions as "excellent" or "good," an improvement from the 8% who said that four years ago, but far from a cheery assessment. And a new poll released this week found higher-income adults are hearing about better economic news than lower-income adults, with 15 percentage point difference between the two groups on the "good news" they're hearing about the job situation, for example.

While most American families remain financially stuck, upper-income families have seen their median wealth double from $318,100 in 1983 to $639,400 in 2013. The typical wealth level of these families increased each decade over the past 30 years. The Great Recession did set back the median wealth of upper-income families, but over the past three years these families have recouped some of their losses.

> *"Income inequality should not be vilified, and public policy should encourage people to move up the income distribution and not penalize them for having already done so."*

Income Inequality Is Not the Problem

Thomas A. Garrett

In the following viewpoint, Thomas A. Garrett argues that statistics showing a rising income gap between the upper-income levels and lower-income levels paint a false picture of income distribution in the U.S. He contends that people's incomes change as they move through their lives. Garrett claims that income inequality is a byproduct of a well-functioning economy. Thomas A. Garrett is an economist previously with the Federal Reserve Bank of St. Louis.

As you read, consider the following questions:

1. What problems does Garrett claim come from using census income statistics to make inferences about income inequality?
2. According to Garrett, how does social mobility affect people's income through their life span?
3. What public policies does Garrett think will positively impact people who live in poverty?

"U.S. Income Inequality: It's Not So Bad," Thomas A. Garrett, Federal Reserve of St. Louis, Spring 2010. Reprinted with permission of the Federal Reserve Bank of St. Louis, www.stlouisfed.org/education.

E ach year, the U.S. Census Bureau releases data on the income levels of America's households. A comparison of the annual data over time reveals that the income of wealthier households has been growing faster than the income of poorer households—the real income of the wealthiest 5 percent of households rose by 14 percent between 1996 and 2006, while the income of the poorest 20 percent of households rose by just 6 percent.

As a result of these differences in income growth, the income of the wealthiest 5 percent of households grew from 8.1 times that of the income of the poorest 20 percent of households in 1996 to 8.7 times as great by 2006. Such figures commonly lead to the conclusion that income inequality in the United States has increased. This apparent increase in income inequality has not escaped the attention of policy makers and social activists who support public policies aimed at reducing income inequality. However, the common measures of income inequality that are derived from the census statistics exaggerate the degree of income inequality in the United States in several ways. Furthermore, although many people consider income inequality a social ill, it is important to understand that income inequality has many economic benefits and is the result of—and not a detriment to—a well-functioning economy.

An Inaccurate Picture

The Census Bureau essentially ranks all households by household income and then divides this distribution of households into quintiles. The highest-ranked household in each quintile provides the upper income limit for each quintile. Comparing changes in these upper income limits over time for different quintiles reveals that the income of wealthier households has been growing faster than the income of poorer households, thus giving the impression of an increasing "income gap" or "shrinking middle class."

One big problem with inferring income inequality from the census income statistics is that the census statistics provide only a snapshot of income distribution in the U.S., at a single point in time. The statistics do not reflect the reality that income for many households changes over time—i.e., incomes are mobile. For most people, income increases over time as they move from their first, low-paying job in high school to a better-paying job later in their lives. Also, some people lose income over time because of business-cycle contractions, demotions, career changes, retirement, etc. The implication of changing individual incomes is that individual households do not remain in the same income quintiles over time. Thus, comparing different income quintiles over time is like comparing apples to oranges, because it means comparing incomes of different people at different stages in their earnings profile.

The U.S. Treasury released a study in November 2007 that examined income mobility in the U.S. from 1996 to 2005. Using data from individual tax returns, the study documented the movement of households along the distribution of real income over the 10-year period. As shown in Figure 1A, the study found that nearly 58 percent of the households that were in the lowest income quintile (the lowest 20 percent) in 1996 moved to a higher income quintile by 2005. Similarly, nearly 50 percent of the households in the second-lowest quintile in 1996 moved to a higher income quintile by 2005. Even a significant number of households in the third- and fourth-lowest income quintiles in 1996 moved to a higher quintile in 2005. The Treasury study also documented falls in household income between 1996 and 2005. This is most interesting when considering the richest households. As shown in Figure 1B, more than 57 percent of the richest 1 percent of households in 1996 fell out of that category by 2005. Similarly, more than 45 percent of the households that ranked in the top 5 percent of income in 1996 fell out of that category by 2005.

Thus it is clear that over time, a significant number of households move to higher positions along the income distribution, and a significant number move to lower positions along the income distribution. Common reference to "classes" of people (e.g., the lowest 20 percent or the richest 10 percent) is quite misleading because income classes do not contain the same households and people over time.

Another problem with drawing inferences from the census statistics is that the statistics do not include the noncash resources received by lower-income households—resources transferred to the households—and the tax payments made by wealthier households to fund these transfers. Lower-income households annually receive tens of billions of dollars in subsidies for housing, food and medical care. None of these are considered income by the Census Bureau. Thus the resources available to lower-income households are actually greater than is suggested by the income of those households as reported in the census data.

At the same time, these noncash payments to lower-income households are funded with taxpayer dollars—mostly from wealthier households, since they pay a majority of overall taxes. One research report estimates that the share of total income earned by the lowest income quintile increases roughly 50 percent—whereas the share of total income earned by the highest income quintile drops roughly 7 percent—when transfer payments and taxes are considered.

The census statistics also do not account for the fact that the households in each quintile contain different numbers of people; it is differences in income across people, rather than differences in income by household, that provide a clearer measure of inequality. Lower-income households tend to consist of single people with low earnings, whereas higher-income households tend to include married couples with multiple earners. The fact that lower-income households have fewer people than higher-income households skews the income distribution by person. When considering household size along with transfers received and taxes paid, the income share of the lowest quintile nearly triples and the income share of the highest quintile falls by 25 percent.

AMERICANS EXPERIENCE INCOME MOBILITY

PSID data show that by age 60:

- 70% of the population will have experienced at least one year within the top 20th percentile of income;
- 53% of the population will have experienced at least one year within the top 10th percentile of income; and
- 11.1% of the population will have found themselves in the much-maligned 1% of earners for at least one year of their lives.
- At the same time, it's much more rare for a person to reach the top 1% and stay there. According to PSID data, only 0.6% of the population will experience 10 consecutive years in the top 1% of earners.

"The myth of the 1% and the 99%," Chris Mathews, *Fortune*, March 2, 2015.

Is Policy Needed?

Income inequality will still exist even if the income inequality statistics are adjusted to account for the aforementioned factors. Given the negative attention income inequality receives in the media, it is important to ask whether reducing income inequality is a worthy goal of public policy. It is important to understand that income inequality is a byproduct of a well-functioning capitalist economy. Individuals' earnings are directly related to their productivity. Wealthy people are not wealthy because they have more money; it is because they have greater productivity. Different incomes reflect different productivity levels.

The unconstrained opportunity for individuals to create value for society—and the fact that their income reflects the value they create—encourages innovation and entrepreneurship. Economic research has documented a positive correlation between entrepreneurship/innovation and overall economic growth. A wary eye should be cast on policies that aim to shrink the income distribution by redistributing income from the more productive to the less productive simply for the sake of "fairness." Redistribution of wealth increases the costs of entrepreneurship and innovation, with the result being lower overall economic growth for everyone.

Poverty and income inequality are related, but only the former deserves a policy-based response. Sound economic policy to reduce poverty would lift people out of poverty (increase their productivity) while not reducing the well-being of wealthier individuals. Tools to implement such a policy include investments in education and job training.

Income inequality should not be vilified, and public policy should encourage people to move up the income distribution and not penalize them for having already done so.

Figure 1A. Movement to Higher Income Quintiles
1996-2005

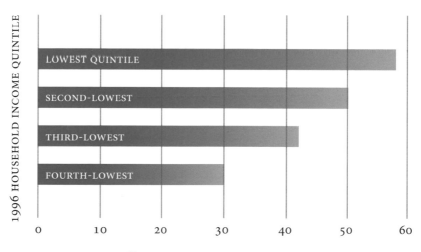

Figure 1B. Movement to Lower Income Group
1996-2005

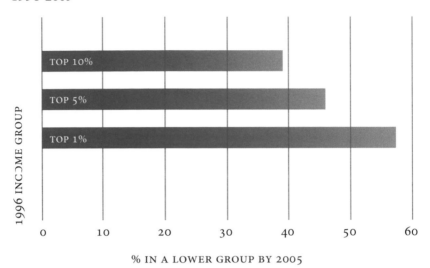

SOURCE: Treasury Department

One problem with popular portrayals of the income gap is that they show income distribution at a single point in time. But for many households, income changes over time. The low-paying jobs from high school days usually give way to better-paying jobs later in life. Figure 1A shows the percentage of households that moved to a higher income quintile from 1996 to 2005. For example, nearly 58 percent of the households in the lowest income quintile in 1996 moved to a higher category by 2005. The reverse also happens, as shown in Figure 1B. Of those households that were in the top 1 percent in income in 1996, for example, more than 57 percent dropped to a lower income group by 2005.

> "The United States scores worse
> mainly because Social Security,
> unemployment insurance, and other
> cash benefits in the United States
> contribute much less to income
> than comparable programs in
> other countries."

US Ranks Last in Income Inequality

Salvatore Babones

In the following article, Salvatore Babones uses the Gini coefficient to make his claim that the U.S. has the highest income inequality compared to 18 other nations who also measure their levels of incomes. He acknowledges that there are problems with using the Gini coefficient to determine household income. Nevertheless, Babones contends that the major reason for the dead-last ranking is the low level of government benefits provided to American families. Babones is a senior lecturer in sociology and social policy at the University of Sydney and an associate fellow at the Institute for Policy Studies.

As you read, consider the following questions:

1. What is the Gini coefficient?
2. According to Salvatore Babones, what does the Gini coefficient show about income inequality in the U.S.?
3. What does the author think are the reasons for the last-place ranking of the U.S. compared to other developed nations?

Levels of income inequality in America today are running at record levels. Activists from the Occupy movement have placed rising inequality firmly on the national agenda, and inequality looks to figure prominently in the 2012 election campaigns.

All this makes inequality statistics suddenly newsworthy, but how do statisticians measure something as slippery as inequality? Some people obviously have more than others, but how does that difference translate into numbers that represent the level of inequality for an entire society?

Anyone following the inequality debate so far has probably heard of the Gini coefficient. America's Gini coefficient is 46.9. Or 37.0. Or may be as high as 57.4. Really, it depends who you ask.

The Gini coefficient was first defined in a 1912 paper by the Italian economist Corrado Gini (1884-1965). The coefficient measures the degree of concentration in a country's income distribution. Social statisticians today use many different inequality measures, but none more than the Gini coefficient.

The Gini coefficient amounts to a kind of percentage and can run from 0 to 100. A Gini of 0 represents 0 percent concentration in a country's income distribution. In a country with a Gini coefficient of 0, everyone receives exactly the same income.

A Gini coefficient of 100 represents 100 percent concentration in a country's income distribution. In a country with a Gini of 100, one person receives all of the country's income. Everyone else gets nothing.

In between 0 and 100, Gini coefficients are harder to interpret. A Gini coefficient of 50 represents 50 percent concentration in a country's income distribution. What does it mean to have 50 percent concentration in a country's income?

A Gini of 50 could mean that half the people share all of the income while the other half get nothing. In other words, a country that literally consisted of haves and have-nots in a 50-50 split would have a Gini coefficient of 50.

This scenario, of course, isn't very realistic. Everyone, no matter how poor, has to have some income to live. There are no literal have-nots.

We could also have a Gini coefficient of 50 with the top 10 percent of a country's population very well-off, the next 50 percent more or less equal, and the bottom 40 percent very poor.

With some fiddling around the edges, that's more or less the situation in America today.

According to the Census Bureau, the official Gini coefficient for the United States was 46.9 in 2010, the most recent year with data available. This is way up from the all-time low of 38.6 set in 1968.

Gini coefficients can be used to measure the concentration of any distribution, not just the distributions of income. Higher concentrations translate into higher inequality. Lower concentrations mean lower inequality,

For example, wealth inequality in America runs much higher than income inequality. New York University economist Edward Wolff estimates the Gini coefficient for household wealth—net worth—in the United States to be 86.5, based on 2009 data. That's much higher than any income inequality estimate.

Leaving aside wealth and other forms of inequality, even income inequality statistics can differ depending on how income is defined.

The most common definition of income used by the Census Bureau and other statistical agencies is total money income of a household, excluding capital gains. All of the members of a household are assumed to share in the household's combined income.

Household income includes wages, salaries, interest, dividends, alimony payments, child support, Social Security payments, and any other cash transfers. It doesn't include food stamps, Medicare, or other non-cash benefits.

A major gap in the measurement of income inequality is the exclusion of capital gains, profits made on increases in the value of investments. Capital gains are excluded for purely practical reasons. The Census doesn't ask about them, so they can't be included in inequality statistics.

Obviously, the rich earn much more from investments than the poor. As a result, real levels of income inequality in America are much higher than the official Census Bureau figures would suggest.

Edward Wolff, working with Federal Reserve Board data that included capital gains, but not government transfer payments, put the figure at 57.4 for 2006.

How does America's Gini coefficient compare to those of other countries? Comparative data on income inequality are reported by the Organisation for Economic Cooperation and Development.

The OECD reports three different Gini coefficients for the United States and other countries (see accompanying table). The first covers the Gini coefficient for wages earned from work. The second traces overall income inequality. The third measures inequality in total living standards, including government-provided health and education benefits.

According to the OECD, the Gini coefficient for income inequality in the United States is just 37.0. The OECD is highly secretive about its methodologies, so it's impossible to know why this is so different from the official figure of 46.9 reported by the U.S. Census Bureau.

Whatever exact procedures the OECD uses, it claims to use the same procedures for all countries. According to the OECD, the Gini coefficient for wages is highest in Italy (46.5) and the United Kingdom (45.6). The United States comes in third-highest out of the 18 developed countries for which data are available.

Gini Coefficients from the Organization for Economic Cooperation and Development

COUNTRY	INEQUALITY IN WAGES EARNED FROM WORK	INCOME EQUALITY (WAGES PLUS OTHER CASH TRANSFERS)	WAGES, TRANSFERS, AND GOVERNMENT-PROVIDED HEALTH & EDUCATION
Australia	41.8	32.4	26.0
Austria	40.6	26.1	21.9
Belgium	40.8	25.6	20.9
Canada	41.6	32.8	25.9
Denmark	37.4	24.3	19.4
Finland	40.3	25.8	21.8
France	43.1	29.2	20.9
Germany	42.0	30.0	24.9
Italy	46.5	33.4	26.2
Luxembourg	43.6	29.2	22.0
Netherlands	39.1	29.7	22.0
Norway	37.6	25.6	19.3
Poland	43.5	31.0	25.9
Portugal	45.8	34.7	29.1
Spain	40.5	31.3	24.8
Sweden	36.8	25.9	18.1
United Kingdom	45.6	34.5	25.2
United States	**45.3**	**37.0**	**30.3**

After other sources of income are included, however, the United States is by far the most unequal of all 18 countries. The United States (37.0) is well ahead of number two Portugal (34.7) and number three United Kingdom (34.5).

The United States scores worse mainly because Social Security, unemployment insurance, and other cash benefits in the United

States contribute much less to income than comparable programs in other countries.

Including the value of government-provided health and education benefits makes the United States look even more unequal compared to other developed countries. In this final comparison the U.S. Gini coefficient (30.3) is still worse than number two Portugal (29.1) and far worse than number three Italy (26.2) and all other developed countries.

By this last measure, the most equal countries in the world are the usual suspects: Denmark (19.4), Norway (19.3), and Sweden (18.1).

So is America's Gini coefficient 46.9 (Census Bureau), 37.0 (OECD), or 57.4 (Edward Wolff based on Federal Reserve data)? It depends what you mean by income. If by income you mean all the money that households get from all sources, including both government transfers and capital gains, then it's probably around 50, give or take a point.

So we're right back to the haves and have-nots. That we're a society of haves and have-nots may not be literally true, but it's more than just a metaphor. America is suspended roughly half-way between full equality and a situation in which all of the country's income is concentrated in one person's hands.

In other words, we're half-way between a socialist utopia and an absolute monarchy. America in 1968 was hardly a socialist country, but it was much closer to the utopia. Maybe it's time to turn back the clock on income inequality. Utopia doesn't sound so bad.

> "*Occupy Wall Street has accomplished what until recently has eluded public health advocates and scientists: it has crystallized a message around the social determinants of health that resonates with broad segments of the population, both domestically and abroad.*"

Income Inequality Has Harmed the 99 Percent

Mary E. Northridge

In the following viewpoint, Mary E. Northridge argues that the Occupy Wall Street movement, which began in 2011, has called attention to the issues surrounding income inequality. She blames several factors for the rise in inequality, such as globalization, technological advances, and stagnation of the minimum wage. She claims that there is a connection between reducing income inequality and improving public health. Northridge is the editor-in-chief of the American Journal of Public Health.

"We Are the 99 Percent," by Mary E. Northridge, American Journal of Public Health, April 2012; 102(4): 585. Published online April 2012. Reprinted by permission of the American Public Health Association.

As you read, consider the following questions:

1. According to Northridge, what are some positive outcomes of the Occupy Wall Street Movement?
2. What does Northridge consider the connection between income inequality and public health?
3. What does Northridge claim has humanized the situations of people who have been harmed by the global financial crisis?

This column is a tribute to the Occupy Wall Street movement for broadening the US national discourse around justice and rights to include income inequality, for fostering solidarity among those who have difficulty providing decent lives for themselves and their families, and for calling attention to the actions of the wealthiest 1% that impoverish the remaining 99% of the population. In the United States, institutions for the protection of the socially and economically vulnerable have historically been shaped by the politics of racial inequality. Now, thanks in large part to Occupy Wall Street, talking explicitly about the 1% and the 99% is not only culturally acceptable, it dominates the public discourse leading into the 2012 presidential campaign season (Freeland C. Inequality, but Without the Villains. *The New York Times*. December 8, 2011. Available at http://www.nytimes.com. Accessed January 27, 2012).

The roots of income inequality are contested and abstract. Market forces, including globalized trade and technological advances, have made highly skilled and well-educated workers more productive, thus increasing their pay. Institutional forces, including deregulation, the decline of unions, and stagnation in the minimum wage, also play a role (http://topics.nytimes.com/top/reference/timestopics/subjects/i/income/income_inequality/index.html?inline=nyt-classifier. Accessed January 27, 2012). On the other hand, Occupy Wall Street has humanized the concept of income inequality and cultivated empathy for those who have been harmed by the ongoing global financial crisis. The Web site,

We Are the 99 Percent (http://wearethe99percent.tumblr.com. Accessed January 27, 2012) posts moving testimonials via hand-written notes of the situations endured by people young and old from all over the world, whose faces are often half-hidden behind their hand-held signs. One reads:

> I'm so happy to know we're in this together. It's been so difficult struggling alone, trying to find a way to get ahead and only falling behind.
>
> The 1% took away our:
> - Democracy
> - Pride
> - Hope.
>
> Let's take it back.
> With interest.
> We deserve it. We are the 99%.

In other words, Occupy Wall Street has accomplished what until recently has eluded public health advocates and scientists: it has crystallized a message around the social determinants of health that resonates with broad segments of the population, both domestically and abroad (Geiger J. Letter to the Editor. *The New York Times*. December 9, 2011. Available at http://www.nytimes .com. Accessed January 27, 2012). Moreover, "the 99 percent" is a group that people are proud to claim as their own, unlike "the poor," and are moved to action in support of its goals of social and economic justice.

Inspired by the rallying cries of protest movements from the Arab Spring to Occupy Wall Street, the theme of National Public Health Week to be observed April 2–8, 2012 is, "A Healthier America Begins Today. Join the Movement!" The emphasis on prevention is laudable, but the message is largely confined to individual actions: eating healthy, avoiding tobacco, receiving vaccinations, and using seat belts (http://www.nphw2012.org/pubs/ NPHW2012_Brochure.pdf. Accessed January 27, 2012). Contrast this advice with the power of the Occupy Wall Street message:

We are the 99 percent. We are getting kicked out of our homes. We are forced to choose between groceries and rent. We are denied quality medical care. We are suffering from environmental pollution. We are working long hours for little pay and no rights, if we're working at all. We are getting nothing while the other 1 percent is getting everything. We are the 99 percent.

In the face of intractable unemployment and economic hardship throughout the United States, public health would do well to underscore the unmistakable public health priorities in the Occupy Wall Street salvo, and work in concert with its allies to promote economic justice and health equity.

> "These changes in family structure, including the growth of single-parent families who tend to be at the lower end of the income distribution, and the growth of two-career high-earner couples near the top end of the income distribution, account for roughly half of the rise in income inequality across households in recent decades."

Powerful Market Shifts Are to Blame for Income Inequality

OpenStax CNX

The following viewpoint argues that the high level of income inequality is caused by two major shifts in the U.S. economy. The author(s) claim that in recent years, high wage earners tend to marry each other, putting their incomes into the highest levels of income. At the other end of the spectrum, a rise in single parent households decreases the bottom level's income. They also contend that increases in technology have produced a winner-take-all labor market. This article is part of a textbook supported by William & Flora Hewlett Foundation, Bill & Melinda Gates Foundation, 20 Million Minds Foundation, Maxfield Foundation, Open Society Foundations, and Rice University.

"Government Policies to Reduce Income Inequality", OpenStax CNX. https://cnx.org/contents/SNSw8gwR@3/Income-Inequality-Measurement. Licensed under CC BY ND 4.0.

As you read, consider the following questions:

1. What are the different methods economists use to measure income inequality?
2. According to the article, how has income inequality changed since the 1970s?
3. What reasons does the article give for the increase in income inequality?

Poverty levels can be subjective based on the overall income levels of a country; typically poverty is measured based on a percentage of the median income. Income inequality, however, has to do with the distribution of that income, in terms of which group receives the most or the least income. Income inequality involves comparing those with high incomes, middle incomes, and low incomes—not just looking at those below or near the poverty line. In turn, measuring income inequality means dividing up the population into various groups and then comparing the groups, a task that can be carried out in several ways, as the next Clear It Up feature shows.

How do you separate poverty and income inequality?

Poverty can change even when inequality does not move at all. Imagine a situation in which income for everyone in the population declines by 10%. Poverty would rise, since a greater share of the population would now fall below the poverty line. However, inequality would be the same, because everyone suffered the same proportional loss. Conversely, a general rise in income levels over time would keep inequality the same, but reduce poverty.

It is also possible for income inequality to change without affecting the poverty rate. Imagine a situation in which a large number of people who already have high incomes increase their incomes by even more. Inequality would rise as a result—but the number of people below the poverty line would remain unchanged.

Why did inequality of household income increase in the United States in recent decades? Indeed, a trend toward greater income inequality has occurred in many countries around the world, although the effect has been more powerful in the U.S. economy. Economists have focused their explanations for the increasing inequality on two factors that changed more or less continually from the 1970s into the 2000s. One set of explanations focuses on the changing shape of American households; the other focuses on greater inequality of wages, what some economists call "winner take all" labor markets. We will begin with how we measure inequality, and then consider the explanations for growing inequality in the United States.

Measuring Income Distribution by Quintiles

One common way of measuring income inequality is to rank all households by income, from lowest to highest, and then to divide all households into five groups with equal numbers of people, known as quintiles. This calculation allows for measuring the distribution of income among the five groups compared to the total. The first quintile is the lowest fifth or 20%, the second quintile is the next lowest, and so on. Income inequality can be measured by comparing what share of the total income is earned by each quintile.

U.S. income distribution by quintile appears in [the following] Table. In 2011, for example, the bottom quintile of the income distribution received 3.2% of income; the second quintile received 8.4%; the third quintile, 14.3%; the fourth quintile, 23.0%; and the top quintile, 51.14%. The final column of [the] Table shows what share of income went to households in the top 5% of the income distribution: 22.3% in 2011. Over time, from the late 1960s to the early 1980s, the top fifth of the income distribution typically received between about 43% to 44% of all income. The share of income that the top fifth received then begins to rise. According to the Census Bureau, much of this increase in the share of income going to the top fifth can be traced to an increase in the share of income going to the top 5%. The quintile measure shows how income inequality has increased in recent decades.

Share of Aggregate Income Received by Each Fifth and Top 5% of Households, 1967–2013

YEAR	LOWEST QUINTILE	SECOND QUINTILE	THIRD QUINTILE	FOURTH QUINTILE	HIGHEST QUINTILE	TOP 5%
1967	4.0	10.8	17.3	24.2	43.6	17.2
1970	4.1	10.8	17.4	24.5	43.3	16.6
1975	4.3	10.4	17.0	24.7	43.6	16.5
1980	4.2	10.2	16.8	24.7	44.1	16.5
1985	3.9	9.8	16.2	24.4	45.6	17.6
1990	3.8	9.6	15.9	24.0	46.6	18.5
1995	3.7	9.1	15.2	23.3	48.7	21.0
2000	3.6	8.9	14.8	23.0	49.8	22.1
2005	3.4	8.6	14.6	23.0	50.4	22.2
2010	3.3	8.5	14.6	23.4	50.3	21.3
2013	3.2	8.4	14.4	23.0	51	22.2

Source: U.S. Census Bureau, Table 2

It can also be useful to divide the income distribution in ways other than quintiles; for example, into tenths or even into percentiles (that is, hundredths). A more detailed breakdown can provide additional insights. For example, the last column of [the] Table shows the income received by the top 5% percent of the income distribution. Between 1980 and 2013, the share of income going to the top 5% increased by 5.7 percentage points (from 16.5% in 1980 to 22.2% in 2013). From 1980 to 2013 the share of income going to the top quintile increased by 7.0 percentage points (from 44.1% in 1980 to 51% in 2013). Thus, the top 20% of householders (the fifth quintile) received over half (51%) of all the income in the United States in 2013.

Lorenz Curve

The data on income inequality can be presented in various ways. For example, you could draw a bar graph that showed the share of income going to each fifth of the income distribution. [The following] Figure presents an alternative way of showing inequality data in what is called a Lorenz curve. The Lorenz curve shows the cumulative share of population on the horizontal axis and the cumulative percentage of total income received on the vertical axis.

The Lorenz Curve

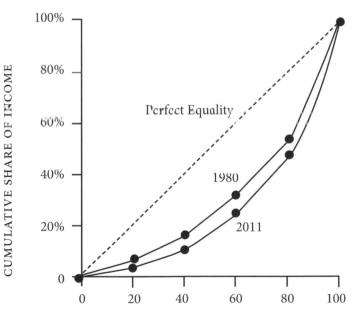

INCOME QUINTILES

Every Lorenz curve diagram begins with a line sloping up at a 45-degree angle, shown as a dashed line in [the figure above]. The points along this line show what perfect equality of the income distribution looks like. It would mean, for example, that the bottom 20% of the income distribution receives 20% of the total income, the bottom 40% gets 40% of total income, and so on. The other lines reflect actual U.S. data on inequality for 1980 and 2011.

The trick in graphing a Lorenz curve is that you must change the shares of income for each specific quintile, which are shown in the first column of numbers in [the table below], into cumulative income, shown in the second column of numbers. For example, the bottom 40% of the cumulative income distribution will be the sum of the first and second quintiles; the bottom 60% of the cumulative income distribution will be the sum of the first, second, and third quintiles, and so on. The final entry in the cumulative income column needs to be 100%, because by definition, 100% of the population receives 100% of the income.

Calculating the Lorenz Curve

INCOME CATEGORY	SHARE OF INCOME IN 1980 (%)	CUMULATIVE SHARE OF INCOME IN 1980 (%)	SHARE OF INCOME IN 2013 (%)	CUMULATIVE SHARE OF INCOME IN 2013 (%)
First quintile	4.2	4.2	3.2	3.2
Second quintile	10.2	14.4	8.4	11.6
Third quintile	16.8	31.2	14.4	26.0
Fourth quintile	24.7	55.9	23.0	49.0
Fifth quintile	44.1	100.0	51.0	100.0

In a Lorenz curve diagram, a more unequal distribution of income will loop farther down and away from the 45-degree line, while a more equal distribution of income will move the line closer to the 45-degree line. The greater inequality of the U.S. income distribution between 1980 and 2013 is illustrated in [the] Figure because the Lorenz curve for 2013 is farther from the 45-degree line than the Lorenz curve for 1980. The Lorenz curve is a useful way of presenting the quintile data that provides an image of all the quintile data at once.

How Does Economic Inequality Vary Around the World?

The U.S. economy has a relatively high degree of income inequality by global standards. As [the following] Table shows, based on a variety of national surveys done for a selection of years in the last five years of the 2000s (with the exception of Germany, and adjusted to make the measures more comparable), the U.S. economy has greater inequality than Germany (along with most Western European countries). The region of the world with the highest level of income inequality is Latin America, illustrated in the numbers for Brazil and Mexico. The level of inequality in the United States is lower than in some of the low-income countries of the world, like China and Nigeria, or some middle-income countries like the Russian Federation. However, not all poor countries have highly unequal income distributions; India provides a counterexample.

COUNTRY	SURVEY YEAR	FIRST QUINTILE	SECOND QUINTILE	THIRD QUINTILE	FOURTH QUINTILE	FIFTH QUINTILE
United States	2013	3.2%	8.4%	14.4%	23.0%	51.0%
Germany	2000	8.5%	13.7%	17.8%	23.1%	36.9%
Brazil	2009	2.9%	7.1%	12.4%	19.0%	58.6%
Mexico	2010	4.9%	8.8%	13.3%	20.2%	52.8%
China	2009	4.7%	9.7%	15.3%	23.2%	47.1%
India	2010	8.5%	12.1%	15.7%	20.8%	42.8%
Russia	2009	6.1%	10.4%	14.8%	21.3%	47.1%
Nigeria	2010	4.4%	8.3%	13.0%	20.3%	54.0%

Income Distribution in Select Countries (Source: U.S. data from U.S. Census Bureau Table 2. Other data from The World Bank Poverty and Inequality Data Base, http://databank.worldbank.org/data/views/reports/tableview.aspx#)

Causes of Growing Inequality: The Changing Composition of American Households

In 1970, 41% of married women were in the labor force, but by 2015, according to the Bureau of Labor Statistics, 56.7% of married women were in the labor force. One result of this trend is that more households have two earners. Moreover, it has become more common for one high earner to marry another high earner. A few decades ago, the common pattern featured a man with relatively high earnings, such as an executive or a doctor, marrying a woman who did not earn as much, like a secretary or a nurse. Often, the woman would leave paid employment, at least for a few years, to raise a family. However, now doctors are marrying doctors and executives are marrying executives, and mothers with high-powered careers are often returning to work while their children are quite young. This pattern of households with two high earners tends to increase the proportion of high-earning households.

According to data in the National Journal, even as two-earner couples have increased, so have single-parent households. Of all U.S. families, 13.1% were headed by single mothers; the poverty rate among single-parent households tends to be relatively high.

These changes in family structure, including the growth of single-parent families who tend to be at the lower end of the income distribution, and the growth of two-career high-earner couples near the top end of the income distribution, account for roughly half of the rise in income inequality across households in recent decades.

Causes of Growing Inequality: A Shift in the Distribution of Wages

Another factor behind the rise in U.S. income inequality is that earnings have become less equal since the late 1970s. In particular, the earnings of high-skilled labor relative to low-skilled labor have increased. Winner-take-all labor markets result from changes in technology, which have increased global demand for "stars,"— whether the best CEO, doctor, basketball player, or actor. This global demand pushes salaries far above productivity differences versus educational differences. One way to measure this change is to take the earnings of workers with at least a four-year college bachelor's degree (including those who went on and completed an advanced degree) and divide them by the earnings of workers with only a high school degree. The result is that those in the 25–34 age bracket with college degrees earned about 1.67 times as much as high school graduates in 2010, up from 1.59 times in 1995, according to U.S. Census data. Winner-take-all labor market theory argues that the salary gap between the median and the top 1 percent is not due to educational differences.

Economists use the demand and supply model to reason through the most likely causes of this shift. According to the National Center for Education Statistics, in recent decades, the supply of U.S. workers with college degrees has increased substantially; for example, 840,000 four-year bachelor's degrees were conferred on Americans in 1970; in 2009–2010, 1,602,480 such degrees were conferred—an increase of about 90%. In [the following] Figure, this shift in supply to the right, from S_0 to S_1, should result in a lower equilibrium wage for high-skilled labor. Thus, the increase in the price of high-skilled labor must be explained by a greater demand, like the movement from D_0 to D_1. Evidently, combining both the increase in supply and in demand has resulted in a shift from E_0 to E_1, and a resulting higher wage.

What factors would cause the demand for high-skilled labor to rise? The most plausible explanation is that while the explosion in new information and communications technologies over the last several decades has helped many workers to become more productive, the benefits have been especially great for high-skilled workers like top business managers, consultants, and design professionals. The new technologies have also helped to encourage globalization, the remarkable increase in international trade over the last few decades, by making it more possible to learn about and coordinate economic interactions all around the world. In turn, the rising impact of foreign trade in the U.S. economy has opened up greater opportunities for high-skilled workers to sell their services

Why Would Wages Rise for High-Skilled Labor?

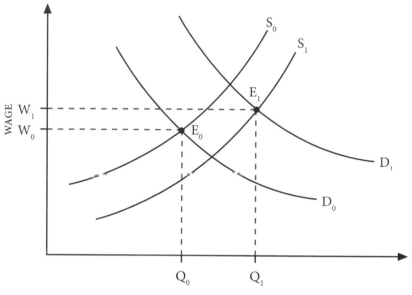

QUANTITY OF HIGH-SKILLED LABOR

around the world. And lower-skilled workers have to compete with a larger supply of similarly skilled workers around the globe.

The market for high-skilled labor can be viewed as a race between forces of supply and demand. Additional education and on-the-job training will tend to increase the supply of high-skilled labor and to hold down its relative wage. Conversely, new technology and other economic trends like globalization tend to increase the demand for high-skilled labor and push up its relative wage. The greater inequality of wages can be viewed as a sign that demand for skilled labor is increasing faster than supply. On the other hand, if the supply of lower skilled workers exceeds the demand, then average wages in the lower quintiles of the income distribution will decrease. The combination of forces in the high-skilled and low-skilled labor markets leads to increased income disparity.

Key Concepts and Summary

Measuring inequality involves making comparisons across the entire distribution of income, not just the poor. One way of doing this is to divide the population into groups, like quintiles, and then calculate what share of income is received by each group. An alternative approach is to draw Lorenz curves, which compare the cumulative income actually received to a perfectly equal distribution of income. Income inequality in the United States increased substantially from the late 1970s and early 1980s into the 2000s. The two most common explanations cited by economists are changes in the structure of households that have led to more two-earner couples and single-parent families, and the effect of new information and communications technology on wages.

Periodical and Internet Sources Bibliography

The following articles have been selected to supplement the diverse views presented in this chapter.

Kurt M. Campbell, "How Income Inequality Undermines U.S. Power," *The Washington Post*, November 30, 2014.

Richard Epstein, "In Praise of Income Inequality," *Defining Ideas,* February 19, 2013.

Nicholas Fitz, "Economic Inequality: It's Far Worse Than You Think," *Scientific American*, March 31, 2015.

Jill Lepore, "Richer and Poorer," *The New Yorker,* March 12, 2015.

Steven J. Markovich, "The Income Inequality Debate," Council on Foreign Relations, February 3, 2014.

Sean McElwee, "Why Income Inequality Is America's Biggest (and Most Difficult) Problem," *Salon*, October 26, 2014.

Deborah Nelson and Himanshu Ojha, "Redistributing Up," *Reuters,* December 18, 2012.

Foon Rhee, "The Numbers Crunch: Income Inequality Gets Worse in America's Cities," *The Sacramento Bee*, January 22, 2016.

Larry Schwartz, "35 Soul-crushing Facts About American Income Inequality," *Salon*, July 15, 2015.

Estelle Sommeiller, Mark Price, and Ellis Wazeter, "Income Inequality in the U.S. by State, Metropolitan Area, and County," Economic Policy Institute, June 16, 2016. http://www.epi.org/publication/income-inequality-in-the-us.

Gillian B. White, "Is America Having the Wrong Conversation About Income Inequality?" *The Atlantic*, April 6, 2016.

OPPOSING
VIEWPOINTS®
SERIES

CHAPTER 2

Is the American Dream Attainable?

Chapter Preface

America is no longer the land of opportunity that it (and others) thinks it is. To a large extent, the American Dream is a myth," writes Noble Prize–winning economist Joseph Stiglitz. His 2016 book, *The Great Divide: Unequal Societies and What We Can Do About Them*, argues that the rising power of the top 1 percent of American earners is leading to unprecedented political and economic inequality. The American Dream of a college education, steady job, and home ownership is increasingly out of reach for most wage earners, say many economists. They point to statistics showing that the incomes of the 1 percent are rising at a healthy rate, while the middle class is losing ground.

Some economists believe that an important cause of the nation's lopsided income distribution is tax policies that advantage the rich. Such policies are presumed to create a dynamic economy in which wealth will "trickle down" to the working classes. According to Stiglitz, in 2016 the top 1 percent took home 20 percent of all pretax income, double the rate of 1980. But because of U.S. tax policies, the country's top earners pay a much lower percent of their income in taxes. The jobs promised by those who cut taxes never materialized, say economists. They were lost to technology or shipped to countries that pay lower wages.

The wealth gap reflects other gaps in society that impact American families, some studies show. Children of low income workers score lower on standardized tests, often because they lack the enrichment that wealthy parents are able to provide. Poor children attend college at lower rates and are saddled with more college debt. Young wage earners have a harder time achieving a higher standard of living than their parents. U.S. Census Bureau statistics show that home ownership in 2016 was at its lowest level in twenty years. Seventy percent of college graduates had student loan debt in 2014.

Wage earners at the lower end of the wealth gap are subject to political and economic policies set for them by a powerful elite who may not represent their interests. They rarely are able to enter the ranks of this elite. This lack of opportunity for disadvantaged workers leads to what Stiglitz calls a "vicious circle" that is reinforced across generations. The United States ranks high among countries with the least amount of social mobility. The advantages or disadvantages parents have tend to be passed on to their children. A new study shows that disparities in education, mental health, obesity, absent fathers, isolation from church, and isolation from community groups are now attributed to growing up rich or poor as much as they are about anything else.

President Barack Obama addressed the dangers of increased inequality in a 2013 speech.

> The combined trends of increased inequality and decreasing mobility pose a fundamental threat to the American Dream, our way of life, and what we stand for around the globe. And it is not simply a moral claim that I'm making here. There are practical consequences to rising inequality and reduced mobility.

Obama pointed out that the consequences of rising inequality affect Americans at all income levels. The authors in this chapter argue various points of view regarding the ability of Americans to attain the American Dream. The pessimists say that the American Dream is dead, killed off by the 1 percent. The optimists claim that the American Dream is alive and well in an economy beginning to grow and thrive again.

| "*The American Dream has become a*
| *nightmare of social stasis.*"

The American Dream Has Ended

Niall Ferguson

In the following viewpoint, Niall Ferguson argues that the American Dream is founded on the ability of hard-working people in lower classes to move upward to higher income levels. Current economic policies, he claims, are preventing such upward mobility. He points out that the United States is now trailing many European countries when comparing upward mobility. Ferguson is a professor of history at Harvard University and a senior fellow at the Hoover Institution and Stanford University.

As you read, consider the following questions:

1. What is the difference between income inequality and social mobility?
2. How does social mobility in the U.S. compare to that of European countries?
3. On what economic policies does Ferguson blame the lack of social mobility in the U.S.?

The United States is where great things are possible." Those are the words of Elon Musk, whose astonishing career illustrates that the American dream can still come true.

Musk was born in South Africa but emigrated to the United States via Canada in the 1990s. After completing degrees in economics and physics at the University of Pennsylvania, he moved to Silicon Valley, intent on addressing three of the most "important problems that would most affect the future of humanity": the Internet, clean energy, and space. Having founded PayPal, Tesla Motors, and SpaceX, he has pulled off an astonishing trifecta. At the age of 42, he is worth an estimated $2.4 billion. Way to go!

But for every Musk, how many talented young people are out there who never get those crucial lucky breaks? Everyone knows that the United States has become more unequal in recent decades. Indeed, the last presidential election campaign was dominated by what turned out to be an unequal contest between "the 1 percent" and the "47 percent" whose votes Mitt Romney notoriously wrote off.

But the real problem may be more insidious than the figures about income and wealth distribution imply. Even more disturbing is the growing evidence that social mobility is also declining in America.

The distinction is an important one. For many years, surveys have revealed a fundamental difference between Americans and Europeans. Americans have a much higher toleration for inequality. But that toleration is implicitly conditional on there being more social mobility in the United States than in Europe.

But what if that tradeoff no longer exists? What if the United States now offers the worst of both worlds: high inequality with low social mobility? And what if this is one of the hidden structural obstacles to economic recovery? Indeed, what if current monetary policy is making the problem of social immobility even worse?

This ought to be grist for the mill for American conservatives. But Republicans have flunked the challenge. By failing to distinguish between inequality and mobility, they have allowed Democrats, in effect, to equate the two, leaving the GOP looking like the party of the 1 percent—hardly an election-winning strategy.

To their cost, American conservatives have forgotten Winston Churchill's famous distinction between left and right—that the left favors the line, the right the ladder. Democrats do indeed support policies that encourage voters to line up for entitlements—policies that often have the unintended consequence of trapping recipients in dependency on the state. Republicans need to start reminding people that conservatism is about more than just cutting benefits. It's supposed to be about getting people to climb the ladder of opportunity.

Inequality and social immobility are, of course, related. But they're not the same, as liberals often claim.

Let's start with inequality. It's now well known that in the mid-2000s the share of income going to the top 1 percent of the population returned to where it was in the days of F. Scott Fitzgerald's Great Gatsby. The average income of the 1 percent was roughly 30 times higher than the average income of everyone else. The financial crisis reduced the gap, but only slightly—and temporarily. That is because the primary (and avowed) aim of the Federal Reserve's monetary policy since 2008 has been to push up the price of assets. Guess what? The rich own most of these. To be precise, the top 1 percent owns around 35 percent of the total net worth of the United States—and 42 percent of the financial wealth. (Note that in only one other developed economy does the 1 percent own such a large share of wealth: Switzerland.)

By restoring the stock market to where it was back before the crisis, the Fed has not achieved much of an economic recovery. But it has brilliantly succeeded in making the rich richer. And their kids.

According to Credit Suisse, around a third of the world's thousand or so billionaires in 2012 were American. But of these, just under 30 percent were not self-made—a significantly higher proportion than for Australia and the United Kingdom. In other words, today an American billionaire is more likely to have inherited his or her wealth than a British one is.

This is just one of many indications of falling social mobility in the U.S. According to research published by the German Institute for the Study of Labor, 42 percent of American men born and raised in the bottom fifth of the income distribution end up staying there as adults, compared with just 30 percent in Britain and 28 percent in Finland. An American's chance of getting from the bottom fifth to the top fifth is 1 in 13. For a British or Finnish boy, the odds are better: more like 1 in 8.

True, the relatively flat income distribution of Scandinavian countries makes it easier to get from the bottom to the top—there's less financial distance to travel. But the same cannot really be said of Britain. Indeed, the amazing thing about the most recent research on social mobility is that the United Kingdom—which used to have the most rigid class structure in the developed world—now risks losing that title to the United States. No wonder Downton Abbey is so popular here.

The American Dream has become a nightmare of social stasis. According to research by Pew, just under 60 percent of Americans raised in the top fifth of incomes end up staying in the top two fifths; a fractionally higher proportion of those born in the bottom fifth—60.4 percent—end up staying in the bottom two fifths.

Perhaps not surprisingly, the child poverty rate is more than double the poverty rate for seniors.

This is the America so vividly described by Charles Murray in his bestselling book Coming Apart. At one end of the social scale, living in places with names like "Belmont," is Murray's "cognitive elite" of around 1.5 million people. They and their children dominate admissions to the country's top colleges. They marry one another and cluster together in fewer than a thousand exclusive neighborhoods—the enclaves of wealth that Murray calls the SuperZips.

At the other end, there are places like "Fishtown," where nobody has more than a high school diploma; a rising share of children live with a single parent, often a young and poorly educated "never-married mother." Not only has illegitimacy risen in such towns,

THE AMERICAN DREAM IS OUT OF REACH

The Red Pin.com suggests the American dream is difficult for the average U.S. family with two children to attain today. The real estate website defines the costs of the American dream as including a mortgage, car payment, gas, utilities, food and water for a family of four, four inexpensive restaurant meals each month for the family, one movie for the family and one date night for the parents, with a three-course meal at a mid-priced restaurant.

"The average U.S. household earning a single average wage, or lower, cannot afford the classic American dream," said Ashley Carlisle of TheRedPin.com. "In fact, the annual average salary is about $10,000 away from reaching that goal and that doesn't even include paying off other debts or investments like retirement or college."

Annual wages of $62,348 are needed to achieve that dream but, in reality, the average American family brings in just $47,598, according to Carlisle.

"That just makes it very difficult, or even impossible, to live out the traditional definition of the dream," she said. "It could suggest that the confines of the traditional American dream may evolve as new generations begin redefining what they consider living a rich and fulfilling life. It may differ from previous generations given these financial constraints."

"Trump Says American Dream Is Dead, Is He Right?" Dora MeKouar, *Voice of America*, **April 25, 2016.**

so has the share of men saying they are unable to work because of illness or disability or who are unemployed or who work fewer than 40 hours a week. Crime is rampant; so is the rate of incarceration. In other words, problems that used to be disproportionately associated with African-American communities are now endemic in the trailer parks and subprime slums inhabited by poor whites. You get born there, you stay there—unless you get sent to jail.

What has gone wrong? American liberals argue that widening inequality inevitably causes falling social mobility. This was what

Alan Krueger, chairman of the Council of Economic Advisers, had in mind back in January, when he came up with the "Great Gatsby Curve," showing that more unequal countries have less social mobility. (Hang on, wasn't Gatsby a self-made bootlegger?) But to European eyes, this is also a familiar story of poverty traps created by well-intentioned welfare programs. Consider the case highlighted by Gary Alexander, Pennsylvania's former secretary of public welfare. A single mom with two young kids is better off doing a part-time job for just $29,000—on top of which she receives $28,327 in various benefits—than if she accepts a job that pays $69,000, on which she would pay $11,955 in taxes.

Another good example is the growth in the number of Americans claiming Social Security disability benefits. Back in the mid 1980s, little more than 1.5 percent of the population received such benefits; today it's nearly 3.5 percent. Nor (as used to be the case) are the recipients mainly elderly. Around 6 percent of the population aged between 45 and 54—my age group—are SSDI beneficiaries. Payments to disabled workers average $1,130 a month, which works out as $13,560 a year—just $2,000 less than a full-time wage at the federal minimum of $7.25 an hour.

Maybe we really are unhealthier than we were 30 years ago, though the data on life expectancy tell a different story. Maybe work really has got more physically demanding, though the shift from manufacturing to services also suggests otherwise. The more credible possibility is that it has become easier for the mildly unwell or unfit to get classified as disabled and to opt for idle poverty over working poverty, which pays only slightly better and means working with that niggling backache or mild depression.

Significantly, after two years on disability benefit, you qualify for Medicare, swelling the ever-growing number of beneficiaries of the federal government's most expensive welfare program. Right now, federal spending on health care, according to the Congressional Budget Office, is around 5 percent of GDP, but it is forecast to double by the 2040s. Needless to say, this reflects the great demographic shift that is inexorably driving up the share of seniors in the population. But consider how the combination of an aging population and welfare programs is working to reduce the resources available to young people.

According to the Urban Institute, the current share of federal spending on the young is around 10 percent, compared with the 41 percent that goes on the non-child portions of Social Security, Medicare, and Medicaid. Per capita government spending—including state and local budgets—is roughly double for the elderly what it is for children. Perhaps not surprisingly, the child poverty rate is more than double the poverty rate for seniors. Ask yourself: how can social mobility possibly increase in a society that cares twice as much for Grandma as for Junior?

The only mystery that remains is why this generational conflict has not yet become a serious issue in American politics. Bafflingly, young voters still tend to line up with the very organizations that seem most intent on ratcheting up the future liabilities of government (not to mention the teenage unemployment rate)—notably the public-sector unions.

Writing in 1960, the economist Friedrich Hayek made a remarkable prediction about the ultimate consequences of the welfare state. "Most of those who will retire at the end of the century," he wrote, "will be dependent on the charity of the younger generation. And ultimately not morals but the fact that the young supply the police and the army will decide the issue: concentration camps for the aged unable to maintain themselves are likely to be the fate of an old generation whose income is entirely dependent on coercing the young."

Hayek was right that by 2000 the baby boomers would expect the young to bear the rising costs of their protracted and generously funded retirements. Almost alone among postwar economists, he saw the generational conflict implied by the welfare state. But he was wrong about how the younger generation would react. Far from rounding up the old and putting them in camps, it is the young who are the docile victims.

One possible explanation for this docility lies in the other main reason for declining social mobility: the disastrous failure of American high schools in the places like Murray's imaginary Fishtown.

Despite a tripling of per-pupil expenditure in real terms, American secondary education is failing. According to the Council on Foreign Relations, three quarters of U.S. citizens between the ages of 17 and 24 are not qualified to join the military because they are physically unfit, have criminal records, or have inadequate levels of education. A third of high school graduates fail the mandatory Armed Services Vocational Aptitude Battery. Two fifths of students at four-year colleges need to take remedial courses to relearn what they failed to master in high school.

In international comparison, the United States is now somewhere in the middle of the league table for mathematical aptitude at age 15. The Organization for Economic Cooperation and Development's most recent Program for International Student Assessment (PISA) study was damning: in math, the gap between the teenagers in the Shanghai district of China and the United States is as large as the gap between American teenagers and Albanians.

But the real shocker is the differential between rich and poor kids. At the ages of 4 to 5, children from the poorest fifth of homes are already 21.6 months behind children from the richest homes in the US, compared with 10.6 months in Canada. The proportion of 15-year-olds who are functionally illiterate (below level 2 in PISA tests) is 10.3 percent in Canada. In the U.S. it is 17.6 percent. And students from the highest social-class groups are twice as likely to go to college than those from the lowest classes.

Meanwhile, there are disturbing signs that America's elite educational institutions are reverting to their old role as finishing schools for the children of a hereditary elite—the role they played back when F. Scott Fitzgerald was partying at Princeton.

In a disturbing critique of Ivy League admissions policies, the editor of the *American Conservative*, Ron Unz, recently pointed out a number of puzzling anomalies. For example, since the mid-

1990s Asians have consistently accounted for around 16 percent of Harvard enrollments. At Columbia, according to Unz, the Asian share has actually fallen from 23 percent in 1993 to below 16 percent in 2011. Yet, according to the U.S. census, the number of Asians aged between 18 and 21 has more than doubled in that period. Moreover, Asians now account for 28 percent of National Merit Scholarship semifinalists and 39 percent of students at CalTech, where admissions are based purely on academic merit.

Perhaps those in charge of Ivy League admissions have good reasons for their decisions. Perhaps it is right that they should do more than simply pick the most academically talented and industrious students who apply. But the possibility cannot be rejected out of hand that, whatever their intentions, the net effect of their pursuit of "diversity" is in fact to reduce yet further this country's once unique social mobility. Nor can we dismiss the hypothesis that the "legacy" system may be the key here, as the cognitive elite discreetly rig the game in favor of their offspring with well-timed benefactions.

As a professor at Harvard, I am disquieted by such thoughts. Unlike Elon Musk, I did not come to the United States intent on making a fortune. Wealth was not my American dream. But I did come here because I believed in American meritocracy, and I was pretty sure that I would be teaching fewer beneficiaries of inherited privilege than I had encountered at Oxford.

Now I am not so sure.

> "America's position on the curve,
> and particularly the relatively low
> rates of upward economic mobility
> of children raised by the lowest
> income households, is caused by
> family dysfunction."

Income Inequality Perpetuates Lower Social Mobility

Miles Corak

In the following viewpoint, Miles Corak uses the "Great Gatsby Curve" to show the relationship between inequality and mobility. He points out that in countries with greater inequality, economic advantages and disadvantages are passed between parents and children. He argues that income inequality lowers social mobility because it reduces opportunities for lower classes to access education. Corak is a professor of economics at the University of Ottowa.

As you read, consider the following questions:

1. What is "the Great Gatsby Curve"?
2. According to Corak, what is the impact of family dysfunction on upward economic mobility?
3. In what ways does Corak believe that America's public policies favor the rich?

"The Great Gatsby Curve: Inequality and the End of Upward Mobility in America," Miles Corak, PBS News Hour, July 15, 2013. Reprinted by permission.

Simone Pathe: Is the American economic system fundamentally unequal, perpetuating income inequality and stymieing upward economic mobility? Or do families—by virtue of their differing genes and values—reproduce income inequality?

In our third in a series of three posts examining economic inequality in America, Miles Corak, professor of economics at the University of Ottawa, uses "The Great Gastsby" metaphor to respond to our two previous posters on this topic: Alan Krueger, President Obama's outgoing chair of the Council of Economic Advisers, who introduced readers to the Great Gatsby Curve on this page on Friday, and Greg Mankiw, who held the same position under George W. Bush, and argued against government redistribution of wealth to create more equality of opportunity on this page on Saturday.

Corak's post for the Making Sen$e page is informed by an article that is forthcoming in the summer issue of the Journal of Economic Perspectives. You can read a draft of the forthcoming article on his website.

Corak uses F. Scott Fitzgerald's Jay Gatsby to explain the competing interpretations of income inequality that we've explored over the past few days on this page. So, as you read, keep this Fitzgerald quote in mind: "The test of a first-rate intelligence is the ability to keep two opposed thoughts in mind at the same time, and still retain the ability to function."

Miles Corak: Was Jay Gatsby, the ambitious hero in F. Scott Fitzgerald's novel, a crook who would stop at nothing to get ahead, or the victim of a crooked game, a system in which the rules are rigged against those with anything other than blue blood, regardless of their ambition? "The Great Gatsby" is certainly open to multiple interpretations, but that is precisely what makes a novel great: characters and plot that not only challenge our deeply held beliefs, but also invite a different perspective depending upon the times we live in.

Fitzgerald's novel has long captured the American imagination because it speaks so directly to the belief that anyone with talent, energy and ambition can succeed regardless of their starting point in life. It has all the more resonance now because inequality has soared in the last three decades.

We re-read "The Great Gatsby," and we re-make the movie, because we wonder if Americans can still make it in a more polarized society where the top 1 percent take home such a large slice of the economic pie, a slice that is matched only by what was happening during the roaring '20s.

While "The American Dream" is probably best left to novelists, this has not stopped economists from trying to put numbers to metaphor.

Is inequality a good thing, reflecting the fruits of skill and ambition and offering a promise of possibility for the next generation? Or does it skew opportunity, crudely mirroring the power of privilege and place and reflecting unfair barriers to success regardless of talent?

It is a fact that countries with greater inequality of incomes also tend to be countries in which a greater fraction of economic advantage and disadvantage is passed on between parents and their children.

It is now common to represent this relationship with what Alan Krueger, the Princeton University economist and out-going Chairperson of the Council of Economic Advisers, has referred to as "The Great Gatsby Curve." Krueger used this term for the first time in a speech given in January 2012, and The White House recently posted an explanatory info-graphic on its website.

The curve ranks countries along two dimensions. Moving horizontally from left to right shows income inequality, as measured about a generation ago, becoming higher and higher across countries. During the early to mid 1980s, Finland, Sweden, Norway and Denmark were the most equal, the United Kingdom and the United States the least.

Moving vertically from bottom to top shows the average degree of stickiness between child adult earnings and the earnings of the family in which children were raised. In countries like Finland,

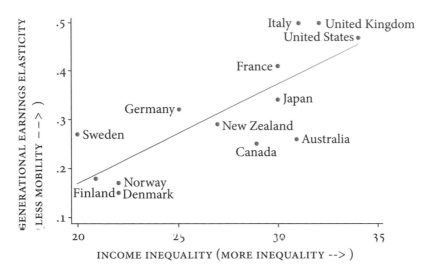

Source: Miles Corak, "Income Inequality, Equality of Opportunity, and Intergenerational Mobility," Journal of Economic Perspectives

Norway and Denmark, the tie between parental economic status and the adult earnings of children is weakest: less than one-fifth of any economic advantage or disadvantage that a father may have had in his time is passed on to a son in adulthood. In Italy, the United Kingdom and the United States, roughly 50 percent of any advantage or disadvantage is passed on.

Does this mean that if you want to live the American Dream, you should move to Denmark? Or could it also mean that taxing the rich and giving to the poor will not only reduce inequality in the here-and-now, but also the degree to which it is passed on to the next generation?

Well, the curve is open to alternative interpretations in part because it is not a causal relationship.

But to dismiss it by simply saying, "correlation does not imply causation," is too glib and risks missing an important message about the underlying causes.

Economic theory predicts such a relationship, and therefore suggests that it is reasonable to juxtapose measures of inequality and mobility as a starting point for understanding the underlying causes and their implications.

Theory also suggests that there is no single driver of this relationship: the interaction between families, labor markets and public policies all structure a child's opportunities and determine the extent to which adult earnings are related to family background—but they do so in different ways across national contexts.

The "Gatsby was a crook" point of view stresses the fundamental role of individual choice, rooted to some important degree in differences in parenting and family values. From this perspective, America's position on the curve, and particularly the relatively low rates of upward economic mobility of children raised by the lowest income households, is caused by family dysfunction.

Single parent families are the underlying driver pushing up the poverty rate, raising the risk of vulnerability for children and undoing any public policies trying to level the playing field. At the same time, top earners are not taking broader social responsibility by championing the values and parenting strategies underlying their own success.

From this perspective, families reproduce inequality, labor market earnings reflect just deserts, and pubic policy is ineffective in changing things. America's position on the Gatsby Curve ultimately reflects more diverse family values—perhaps rooted even in a more diverse genetic make-up—than in other countries.

The "Gatsby was a victim of a crooked system" point of view suggests that a more polarized labor market is the main driver, eventually being shadowed in the capacities of parents to invest in their children's future, and even in family structure and values.

Parents with more education invest more in their children, and in an era of rising labor market inequality, not only do they have more resources, they have a much stronger incentive to see that their children in turn develop the skills that will lead to success.

Globalization and technical change have not only raised the returns to a good education, they have also implied that wages have been stagnant, and even falling, among less skilled parents, putting extra strains on their families. Having to run harder just to stand still, these families not only have less money for their children's future, but also less time. The chances that marriages last, and indeed the economic incentives to even get married, are more troublesome when good jobs and good wages don't offer the same bedrock they once did.

On top of all this, public policy is designed to favor the relatively well-to-do. Access to high quality early childhood education and primary schools is limited to those with wealth. Their children are put on the direct path to the best colleges, offering a gateway to labor market success.

From this perspective, America's position on the curve is the result of rising returns to schooling and declining access to good jobs, a trend that has been much stronger in the United States than elsewhere. With more inequality, public policy choices are also skewed, particularly in institutions fostering human capital development like education and health care, to tilt rather than to level the playing field.

Social science doesn't always give us hard-and-fast truths, but it does give us more than metaphor. And while even agreed upon facts can be legitimately viewed as having different meanings, we should be clear that the message underlying the Gatsby Curve is that inequality may lower mobility because it has the potential to shape opportunity.

The curve is telling us that inequality heightens the income consequences of innate and other family-based differences between individuals; that inequality also changes opportunities, incentives and institutions that form, develop and transmit characteristics and skills valued in the labor market; and that inequality shifts the balance of power so that some groups are in a position to structure policies or otherwise support their children's achievement independent of talent.

America's position on the Gatsby Curve calls, as a result, for a careful second reading of the configuration of these forces to fully appreciate both the benefits and the costs of higher inequality.

> "*Since the Great Depression, the American Dream has been linked to homeownership. Now, … America is well on the road to becoming a renter nation.*"

Downward Mobility Is the New Normal

Mechele Dickerson

In the following viewpoint, Mechele Dickerson argues that three trends in the American economy point to the death of the American Dream. She claims that housing is unaffordable, wages are stagnant, and older Americans are unable to save for retirement. She contends that American despair over achieving financial security is producing alarming consequences for lower- and middle-income white Americans. Dickerson is a professor of law at the University of Texas at Austin.

As you read, consider the following questions:

1. According to Dickerson, how are housing trends reflecting the loss of the American Dream?
2. According to Dickerson, what is the situation of Americans nearing retirement?
3. What are some physical signs of the economic anxiety felt by lower- and middle-class white Americans?

The American Dream that has existed in this country for over 50 years is on life support. For some Americans, it may already be dead.

While recent consumer confidence surveys indicate that Americans seem somewhat optimistic about the overall economy, most polls and studies show that we are anxious about our own economic futures. Many Americans no longer seem to believe that they will ever be financially secure or stable. The belief that you can succeed financially with hard work and determination has been a core tenet of the American Dream. Now more than three-quarters of all Americans believe that downward mobility is more likely than upward mobility.

Are the foundational elements of our collective dream and middle-class lifestyle—owning a home, having stable employment and retiring debt-free and financially secure—now out of reach for most of us, especially the young? And has the problem of the vanishing middle class now reached a group that had seemed entrenched, suburban white Americans?

I've been researching these themes recently while writing a book on the topic. In part I'm trying to understand what these disturbing trends—including stagnant wages and runaway debt— mean for the American Dream, a term first coined by writer James Truslow Adams 85 years ago:

> that dream of a land in which life should be better and richer
> and fuller for everyone, with opportunity for each according
> to ability or achievement.

Let's examine the three tenets above and see if they can still support the "dream of our land."

Housing is Unaffordable

Since the Great Depression, the American Dream has been linked to homeownership. Now, almost 10 years after the worst economic crisis since the '30s, America is well on the road to becoming a renter nation.

While the cost of buying basic staples (like food and clothing) has largely remained the same or dropped over the last 30 years, housing prices have soared, especially during the housing boom in the early 2000s. (Prices fell during the 2007-2009 recession, but they have since recovered and are rising in many regions in the country.)

As prices rise, homeownership rates are going in the opposite direction. After peaking at almost 70 percent in 2004 during the housing boom, they've plunged, falling to below a 50-year-low of below 64 percent in 2015.

As homeownership rates have dropped, the number of renter households has grown. In fact, renter households are now the majority in nine of the 11 largest U.S. metropolitan areas. Renting is no longer limited to recent high school or college graduates as the majority of renters in the country are 40 years or older, up from 43 percent in 1995.

While no state, county or major city in the United States has enough affordable housing for its poorest residents, it's not just those families who are forced to rent. Even Americans employed full-time are now struggling to find affordable rental housing, in part because demand has surpassed the supply of such units, causing rental prices to rise.

Just a decade ago, these middle-income families might have become homeowners, but now they are putting pressure on the rental market because they can't afford to buy. That leaves fewer affordable rental homes or apartments for everyone else.

One of the primary reasons families cannot afford to buy homes or find affordable rental housing is that housing costs have risen quicker than household income.

Downward Economic Mobility

The fact is that for all but the highest-paid workers, wages have been stagnant for almost 30 years. In addition, American workers must now contend with an unstable and unsteady labor market.

While unemployment rates are now below 5 percent, well below the historically high rates during the Great Recession, all but the best-paid workers routinely experience multiple, sustained periods of unemployment. Likewise, workers are now more likely to be under-employed and hold jobs that require less training or education than they have. Also, workers are more likely to hold more than one job at a time and quilt a "patchwork of paychecks" together just to make ends meet.

Stagnant wages and unsteady employment have helped create income and wealth inequality gaps that are now approaching levels this country has not seen in almost a century. Because the richest Americans are receiving a disproportionate share of income and wealth in the U.S., the American Dream of upward mobility from the lower to the middle-class has all but vanished.

And some even argue that generational mobility is now more likely in some European countries than it is in the U.S.

Because wages have not kept pace with soaring housing prices in most places in this country, Americans must now make trade-offs and sacrifices.

One-fifth of all employed Americans must find ways to supplement their income just to pay bills and buy groceries. Fourteen percent are spending more on their credit cards to pay for their monthly living expenses, and 17 percent of workers have been forced to sacrifice their retirement security.

Retirement Insecurity and Instability

Things look bleak for those Americans nearing retirement. As for young adults, financial security during their sunset years seems almost hopeless.

Federal Reserve data show that 31 percent of people who have not yet retired and 19 percent of 55-64-year-old adults who are nearing retirement age have no postwork savings or private pension.

Older baby boomers who either have retired or are approaching retirement often find that they have inadequate savings even though

AMERICAN DREAM IS THREATENED

On December 4, President Obama gave an important speech about inequality and economic mobility in the United States. The speech included some striking data and references to key studies, and makes a set of arguments for the need to address inequality and mobility:

- Since 1979, the nation's productivity has gone up by more than 90 percent, but the income of the typical family has increased by less than eight percent. Our economy has more than doubled in size, but most of that growth has flowed to a fortunate few.
- The top 10 percent no longer takes in one-third of our income—it now takes half.
- The gap in test scores between poor children and wealthy children is now nearly twice what it is between white children and black children.
- A child born into a low-income home will hear 30 million fewer words than a child from a well-off family by the time he or she turns 3 years old, which means by the time he or she starts school they are already behind, and that deficit can compound itself over time.

"Trends of Increasing Inequality and Decreasing Mobility Pose a Threat to the American Dream," by Mark Greenberg, Administration for Children & Families, published on December 18, 2013.

many of them worked for employers who provided traditional pensions rather than 401(k)-styled employee-funded individual savings plans.

Americans coming into retirement are also burdened with more housing, automobile and even student loan debts than people their age did a decade ago.

As a result, many baby boomers have decided to push back their retirement date.

Younger Americans are also struggling to save for retirement. Young adults lack retirement savings because many of them are part-time workers who do not have access to a plan that sets aside some of their pay or because they are too burdened with student loan and other debts to be able to save for retirement.

The Death of the Dream

Americans who have worked hard and played by the rules now fear that they will never be financially successful.

They have lost faith in the American Dream. They are disillusioned, and they are showing signs of despair.

Both conservative working-class Americans who do not have a college degree and ultra-liberal college-educated millennials are displaying their anger in this presidential election cycle.

Many voters who have lost faith in the American Dream are embracing nontraditional populist candidates like Bernie Sanders and Donald Trump. Disenchanted and disaffected voters seem willing to support extreme views and proposals because they no longer believe that traditional political candidates will find a way to create secure jobs that pay decent wages and help move the working class into the middle class.

One group in particular—whites aged 45 to 54 without a college degree—appears to have given up on the American Dream. White noncollege Americans, especially males, no longer seem to believe that hard work and determination is enough to achieve financial success.

They blame politicians, particularly President Obama, for pushing economic policies that harm the middle class. They are anxious, they are angry and they doubt that their high school diploma or work skills will be enough for them to succeed in the job market.

Disturbing physical signs of this economic anxiety includes increased first-time heroin use by whites, particularly young males, shortened average lifespans and their rising suicide rates.

While the American Dream of upward mobility and financial security is alive and well for the richest Americans, lower- and middle-income Americans have never felt less secure financially than they do now.

Downward mobility is now the new normal for most Americans. Upward mobility is now an almost insurmountable dream.

> *"Groundbreaking research by a group of academics has found that, in fact, the dream is quite alive in the United States."*

The American Dream Isn't Always a Dream

Ronald A. Wirtz

In the following article, Ronald A. Wirtz claims that the American Dream is alive and well in certain areas of the country. He finds that communities with a strong economy have high intergenerational income mobility. Other factors that are associated with upward mobility are integrated neighborhoods, high school performance, and strong community organizations. This article first appeared in the October 2014 issue of the fedgazette, *a regional business and economics publication from the Federal Reserve Bank of Minneapolis. Wirtz is the editor of* fedgazette.

As you read, consider the following questions:

1. What does the author mean by a community's "social capital"?
2. According to Wirtz, what are some factors associated with upward mobility in a community?
3. What is the impact of education on a community's upward mobility?

"Movin' on Up," Ronald A. Wirtz, October 22, 2014, Federal Reserve Bank of Minneapolis/fedgazette. This article first appeared in the October 2014 issue of the fedgazette, a regional business and economics publication. Reprinted with permission of the Federal Reserve Bank of St. Louis www.stlouisfed.org/education.

The Quick Take: *Upward income mobility—children faring better financially than their parents—is widely believed to be stagnant, even decreasing in the United States. New research by a team of academics has found that, in fact, the American dream is still alive, but achieving it depends heavily on where you grow up.*

In large swaths of the country, upward income movement across generations is low. But if you live in the Ninth District, statistically speaking, you're more upwardly mobile than people living elsewhere in the country. The reasons for this are hard to pinpoint, but appear to stem, at least in part, from comparatively better education outcomes, greater family stability, strong local economies that foster a larger middle class and access to good-paying jobs, whether in oilfields or in larger cities where wages are higher. In rural areas, the strength of the farm economy—as well as its cyclicality—also appears to play a role in improving the fortunes of children compared with their parents.

Few notions are as ingrained in the national psyche as the American dream—the idea that kids will be better off than their parents and that anybody can make it to the top in this country with a little grit, determination and hard work, no matter their starting place on the ladder.

But there is national hand-wringing over the state of the dream—a victim of income inequality, a sluggish economy coming off a horrendous recession or sundry other factors. A *Wall Street Journal*/NBC poll in early August found that "Americans are registering record levels of anxiety about the opportunities available to younger generations." A CBS poll in early summer reported that almost three in five believed that "the American dream has become impossible for most people to achieve."

Bruce Vold has a multigenerational perspective on the matter. The pastor at Trinity Lutheran Church in Carrington, N.D., he's a third-generation churchman who has lived the American dream even if that was never the goal. Vold's pastor grandfather was paid "in chicken" in the 1930s—rather than receiving a salary, parishioners would give him chickens or "a cow for milk for a family of seven. They had nothing," Vold said. But each successive generation has attained a higher standard of living.

Vold and his wife, Anne, have three children: two out of college and one still attending. "Certainly, we wanted them to have professional success," said Vold. "But I didn't care what they did. ... I'm looking more for how they are contributing to society."

Nonetheless, the young Vold clan appears poised to continue the sought-after American dream of moving up financially. Middle child Matthew has a business degree and works at Dakota Growers, a large pasta plant in his hometown. Daughter Kelly is studying dentistry at Concordia College in Moorhead, Minn.

Eldest son Bryan is an accountant in Minneapolis. He also attended Concordia College, and "didn't have a clue" about what he wanted to be until he took a sophomore class in accounting in 2006. With the Great Recession looming, "accounting looked like [a career that] I should be able to get a good job in," he said. He was right, landing a position at tax and audit giant Grant Thornton before the start of his senior year. After five years, he now makes about $70,000 annually.

Regarding his financial prospects, "I always felt I would do better" than his parents in terms of income, but not because of a poor upbringing, said Bryan. Growing up, "we didn't lack for anything, but there wasn't any excess."

The Vold kids also heard about the importance of going to college—not so much for careers and big money, but to obtain a broad world view and "to learn how to learn," said Bruce Vold. "I think I'm a frugal person and try to be wise about things and feel good about getting my kids through college. ... But they are going to do better financially."

One family's story cannot capture the national experience when it comes to intergenerational income mobility—how kids fare financially compared with their parents. But reports of the death of upward income mobility in this country may be exaggerated. Groundbreaking research by a group of academics has found that, in fact, the dream is quite alive in the United States.

However, the research also unearthed a major caveat: It matters where you grow up. In large swaths of the country, upward income mobility is low. But if you live in the Ninth District, statistically speaking, your upward mobility is much higher and rivals anywhere in the country. The reasons for this are hard to pinpoint, but appear to stem, at least in part, from comparatively better education outcomes, greater family stability, strong local economies that foster a large middle class and proximity to and availability of good jobs in oilfields and higher-paying metro areas. In rural areas, the strength of the farm economy—as well as its cyclicality—also appears to play a role in how children do financially compared with their parents.

That's not to say that everyone, everywhere in the Ninth District is upwardly mobile. Some places, particularly Indian reservations, continue to experience generational poverty and income stagnation. But even these places have a unique story to tell regarding the quality of life where people call home.

The Research Base

Recently, a group of academic researchers led by Raj Chetty of Harvard University released a comprehensive study on the intergenerational income mobility of poor families nationwide. (See Chetty, Hendren, Kline and Saez 2014. NBER Working Paper 19843.) All of the data in this study were made public, serving as the foundation for this *fedgazette* analysis.

The research—which has evolved into an ongoing study called the Equality of Opportunity Project—looked at the incomes of children from the poorest families to see how these children later fared as 30- to 32-year-olds. Subjects in the study, who were identified anonymously through federal tax records, were then grouped into commuting zones, or clusters of counties with strong commuting ties that serve as a rough proxy for regional economies nationwide. The study found that upward income mobility, while generally lower in the United States than in many developed countries, hasn't changed much. But the researchers found major differences in income mobility depending on where children grew up. In Atlanta, for example, only 4.5 percent of children from households in the lowest 20 percent of income can expect to be in the top 20 percent as adults. In Rochester, Minn., and Fargo, N.D., it's 14 percent, which compares favorably with high-mobility countries around the world.

"We actually came in just asking a simple question of whether the American dream is still alive and whether the U.S. is a land of opportunity, and what we found is that that question really doesn't have a straightforward answer because the answer seems to depend very much on geography. That is, it depends on where you grew up," said Chetty earlier this year in St. Cloud, Minn., where he was giving a speech at St. Cloud State University. "In some parts of the U.S., kids who grow up at the bottom of the income distribution, in disadvantaged families, end up having very high chances of moving up ... and in other places the American dream doesn't seem to be nearly as alive."

Enter the Ninth District, where adult children in the study scored much higher on two fundamental measures of income mobility analyzed by the *fedgazette*: absolute upward mobility and bottom-to-top mobility. This performance was not a methodological quirk—something driven by, say, the Bakken oil boom and a red-hot North Dakota economy. Every district state outperformed the nation as a whole in both measures, often by considerable margins.

For absolute upward mobility, the distribution of the district's 87 commuting zones shifts far to the right, or up the income mobility ladder, compared with 622 other commuting zones across the country. At the same time, the chances of going from rags to riches—from the bottom quintile of income to the top—were also higher in the district.

We're #1 (through #6)

The district is home to many of the nation's highest income mobility commuting zones. North Dakota alone grabbed the top six scores in absolute upward mobility in the country, and seven of the top eight. Two of these are located in the western oil patch, a region that has seen unprecedented income gains over the past decade. But the other five are rural commuting zones located outside the Bakken region.

Both opportunities and obstacles abound on reservations looking for more economic activity.

One of them is the Carrington area, home to the Volds, located in the heart of the state and encompassing Foster and Eddy counties. The commuting zone is ranked eighth nationally in absolute upward mobility, but doesn't necessarily look or feel rich in the way you might expect in a place reported to be upwardly mobile. Until about 2010, the city's population had been in gradual decline and has increased by only a few dozen people since then, according to the U.S. Census Bureau. Homes lining the streets, and the vehicles plying them, are like a new pair of comfortable shoes: nice, functional, but not gaudy. There is wealth in the community, numerous sources said, but it is not often publicly displayed.

Income mobility rankings by the Chetty research team do not solely depend on the net change or difference in the income of children versus that of parents (see methodology sidebar). Nonetheless, income gains are a decent predictor. In Foster and Eddy counties, for example, annual median income for the adult children rose to $61,500, up from $53,000 (inflation-adjusted) for their parents.

Carrington, which sits at the intersection of two major state highways, feels like a city of more than 2,100 people. There's a new hotel in town, and Central City Grain is erecting an 820,000-bushel steel bin to match the slightly smaller one it put up two years ago. The streets in many places are a mess—not because of neglect, but because they are being torn out and replaced, thanks to a new

1 percent increase in the local sales tax. The city boasts 50 to 60 job openings, and that's only the advertised jobs.

Vold said the growing affluence in the community can be seen in the parking lots. "We're not in the suburbs of Minneapolis or St. Paul or wherever ... but the number of newer pickups that kids drive and park in the school parking lot" seems to be growing, he said.

On a map, Carrington is an island in a sea of agriculture, 45 minutes by car from Jamestown (pop. 15,000) and two hours from Fargo, Bismarck and Minot. That seeming isolation has its advantages. Two decades ago, the city beat out almost 30 other communities competing for the Dakota Growers plant, which employs about 200. The community's central location and its good highway and rail access were factors in the firm's decision to build in Carrington.

Today, Agro-Culture Liquid Fertilizer is building a new plant in Carrington "because they can distribute to a four-state area from here and save themselves a lot of money," said James Linderman, Carrington economic development director. "So that's been a really big help for us—our geographical location within the state and what's around us."

Don't Forget the Big Cities

Larger cities in the Ninth District also fared well among their peers. St. Cloud scored highest among 381 metropolitan statistical areas nationwide in absolute upward mobility; several others were in the top 25, and all 15 MSAs in the district ranked in the top quartile.

These results were something of a revelation to some observers, such as King Banaian, a St. Cloud resident and state representative in the Minnesota House. "It did surprise me to some extent," he said. Nonetheless, Banaian had no problem offering possible explanations for the ranking, in part because he's an economist and interim dean at the School of Public Affairs Research Institute at St. Cloud State University (SCSU) and co-author of the St. Cloud Quarterly Business Report.

St. Cloud might not have the upper income potential of the Twin Cities, he said, but the city has always had good places to work. The region has a higher-than-average percentage of manufacturing jobs, at 15 percent, and many are in high-value sectors like technology and precision instruments.

While the region has lost manufacturing jobs, the overall rate of job loss from 2003 to 2013 (6.5 percent) was significantly lower than the statewide average (10.8 percent) over this period. At the same time, the area has seen strong growth in other sectors like health care. The region is a medical center for much of the north-central part of the state, Banaian noted.

Banaian also believes that St. Cloud's proximity to the Twin Cities, roughly an hour away, is a big reason for the ranking. Minneapolis-St. Paul is a big draw for St. Cloud residents. That matters because the Chetty research team assigned all income of the adult children to their home commuting zone when they were 16 years old. So in the study's statistical framework, St. Cloud children who left home for the bright lights of Minneapolis nonetheless had their paychecks attributed back to their home commuting zone.

"We're just a way-stop to the Twin Cities," Banaian said. "Our number one export is smart kids." The department recently found that of roughly 700 alumni, 400 lived in the Twin Cities. "Most probably went down there to earn more money than they could get here."

Many sources in other communities similarly acknowledged that their sons and daughters had gone elsewhere to make their living, very often to larger cities that historically have paid higher wages, thus offering a better opportunity to surpass mom and dad's income.

Vold is not even the sole pastor at Lutheran Trinity whose children went away for college and later found good jobs in bigger cities. His colleague, Russ Christiansen, grew up 35 miles away in the little town of McHenry. He and his wife of 38 years have two kids; a daughter lives in South St. Paul, Minn., and does administrative work out of her home for a hospital based in Duluth. Their son works in Fargo for Microsoft and "earns more than my wife and I together," said Christiansen.

Of course, no community keeps all of its own, and young adults from every community move away to find their fortune. But higher upward mobility in the district might also be related to comparatively high college attainment in district states; North Dakota and Minnesota rank among the top seven states for percentage of adults ages 25 to 64 with an associate's degree or higher, and South Dakota and Wisconsin are above the national average, according to Census figures. Such attainment makes it more probable that hometown kids will land higher-paying jobs in professional fields, whether at home or elsewhere.

In Carrington, "I see the expectation of the student [to achieve] from the parents, from the community, from the school," said Brian Duchscherer, superintendent of Carrington Public Schools. He said that 86 percent of the high school class of 2013 had plans to pursue two-year or four-year degrees. "Combine that with the economic climate in North Dakota right now ... [and] I think it's the perfect storm when those two meet."

More on Why and How

Ultimately, the factors behind intergenerational income mobility are many and vary by location. But it's not hard to infer why some commuting zones have high income mobility.

For example, the commuting zone of Dickinson, N.D.,—which includes the counties of Stark (home to Dickinson), Billings and Dunn—has the highest absolute upward mobility ranking in the country. While there is no irrefutable proof, its location in the Bakken oilfields likely plays a considerable role in its high rank.

In 2013, for example, 47 percent of the 22,000 jobs in Stark and Dunn counties, and 67 percent of income earned, were related to the oil and gas industry, according to a recent report by Job Service North Dakota. (Figures for much smaller Billings County were unavailable.)

In the Chetty study, average annual income for adult children in the Dickinson commuting zone was almost $76,000 in 2011-12 (current dollars); that compares with about $65,000 for parents in this zone (1996-2000 average, adjusted for inflation to 2012 dollars).

But in other places, as well as more broadly across states, teasing out the reasons for high or low upward mobility is a very complex task because a multitude of economic and social factors influence income over generations. Rank could even be influenced by methodology.

Robert Johnson, professor and chair of the Ethnic Studies and Pre-College departments at SCSU, suggested to Chetty after his speech in St. Cloud that the city's top ranking in absolute upward mobility among MSAs might be influenced by the timing of the parent sample. By choosing to study children born in 1980 to 1982 and measuring income of the parents in the latter half of the 1990s, the St. Could population sample "at the time, would have had low ethnic and minority populations," who typically fared worse on mobility measures nationwide.

Over the past two decades, St. Cloud has seen a considerable increase in immigrant—particularly Somali—and domestic minority populations, according to Johnson. Whether these new St. Cloud residents will experience similarly high mobility, "you'll have to wait another 10 to 15 years for those results."

While the Chetty research team did not specifically factor for demographic changes in local population samples, it did investigate a number of variables looking for correlations to mobility—not causal proof, but evidence that the presence (or absence) of a particular factor was common to those with high (or low) upward mobility. Among almost three dozen variables studied, five stood out for having a significant correlation with income mobility: residential segregation, size of the middle class, K-12 test scores, social capital and single parenthood.

As one might expect given their high mobility rankings, Ninth District commuting zones generally outperformed the nation on these measures. Residential segregation, which includes income and racial segregation, is lower in many district communities. This might be partly due to the fact that many district commuting zones are smaller in population (which tends to limit the upper end of the income distribution) and largely white (reducing racial segregation by default).

Other correlations also offer a notable contrast compared with the rest the country. For example, the middle class—defined as the percent of parents with incomes between the 25th and 75th percentile of the national income distribution—is larger in Ninth District commuting zones, while the fraction of children living with single mothers is smaller. As for school performance, income-adjusted school test scores in English and math for children in third through eighth grades tend to be uniformly higher.

Ninth District commuting zones also tend to have higher social capital, which the Chetty team gauged through voter turnout, percentage who return Census forms and participation in community organizations. Upwardly mobile St. Cloud offers a good example.

"There is tremendous social capital here. ... People are willing to invest their time, talent and treasure into the community. And you can see it," said Banaian. He pointed to the renovation of Lake George and Eastman Park near downtown, which had fallen into disrepair. In 2007, the St. Cloud Rotary Club raised over $1.5 million from local businesses and members, which helped leverage a total investment of $7 million to transform the lake and park into a community destination with walking and biking trails, sitting areas, fishing piers, a splash park and meeting facilities.

In 2011, the club started hosting "Summertime by George," a weekly festival at the park featuring live music, a farmers market, food vendors and family activities. Attendance reached 86,000 people in the summer of 2013, and Rotary members logged 1,500 volunteer hours.

"It's the biggest thing in town. This is like a party on steroids," said Banaian. "If you're looking for anyone on Wednesday night, they are down there."

Back Home on the Farm

The Chetty research team looked at only a few isolated factors directly related to local economies, including the share of manufacturing jobs and workforce participation rates, and found no strong correlations. An exhaustive review of other local-economy factors—like employment growth and industry mix—is outside the scope of the project. But there does appear to be one factor— identified by multiple sources and supported by data—that seems likely to have influenced upward mobility rankings, particularly for lightly populated rural areas: agriculture.

In this case, the time frame for measuring the income of parents (1996 to 2000) came when the farm economy in many ag-dependent counties was poor to modest, but was followed by one of the strongest farm economies of recent memory. The ag surge appears to have had significant spillover effects.

For example, the commuting zone of Linton, N.D., includes the counties of Emmons, Logan and McIntosh, with a combined population of just 8,200. The zone ranks second in the country in absolute upward mobility, but that's not necessarily obvious in the zone's biggest city—Linton, population 1,100. Broadway Street downtown is active, but also has a few vacant storefronts and has lost some business anchors over the years, according to local sources. The town of tidy neighborhoods and unassuming, well-maintained houses appears content with what it has, rather than dreaming about what it might become.

Without a vibrant farm economy, it's difficult to see how this commuting zone could be ranked so high, and the study's timing likely plays a role as well. In the late 1990s, farming in the region was struggling, responsible for just 13 percent of the three-county economy, according the Bureau of Economic Analysis; in 1997, annual net farm income in this region averaged less than $25,000 per farm (unadjusted for inflation), including fairly generous government subsidies, according to the USDA's Census of Agriculture.

Things didn't improve quickly, but a confluence of factors over the next decade and a half—rising commodity prices, higher yields from better farm practices and movement to more profitable commodities like corn and soybeans—eventually led to record farm income in the region (and across North Dakota). By 2012, annual average net farm income had risen to almost $120,000 per farm in these three counties, and agriculture's share of total personal income in this commuting zone leapt to 42 percent.

Spencer Larson is a recently retired senior farm loan officer for the USDA's Farm Service Agency in Linton. He came to Linton in 1972 to work for the Farmers Home Administration (renamed the Farm Service Agency in the 1990s). Over a 42-year career, Larson has ridden the agricultural roller coaster with local farmers, including the brutal 1980s, when many farmers went bankrupt.

Things started turning around in the 1990s, Larson said, thanks to more consistent precipitation, better farming techniques and technology. Eventually, farmers started making real money, and some weren't quite sure what to do, Larson said. "One young farmer said, 'You know, now that I'm making money, it's more stressful on my wife and [me] because we have to decide where to spend it instead of giving it all back to the lender.'"

He knows of one young man who came back to the area to farm. "His dad gave him a nice part of his unit to farm, gave him all of the equipment—he just had to borrow money for the inputs and the rent." Despite fairly high rent that first year, Larson said, "the kid … hit the crop, hit the price and he was on his way … from basically nothing to six-figure [net worth]. In less than 10 years of farming, he probably has equity in excess of $1 million today."

For some, the hardscrabble days seem like ancient history. "I'm on the third or fourth generation of farmers," Larson said. "The dads that have turned over [operations] to their sons and daughters have said, 'My kids have never experienced a bad year. I'm worried what's going to happen when that happens.' We've had no crisis, no severe weather issues, no overall big disasters," but he added that current low crop prices would be a big test for young farmers.

While farm consolidation continues, new opportunities have opened up in the farm economy, according to Larson and multiple other sources. For example, agronomy—the science and technology of food production and farm management—has brought new companies and jobs to town, helping farmers with soil science, irrigation, weed and pest control, crop rotation and more. Many agronomy jobs involve considerable schooling, bringing jobs for college graduates to many rural communities. "So that's been a job opportunity that was nonexistent 20 years ago," said Larson.

Thriving agriculture also offers a chance for sons and daughters to come home. While there are no good data on such matters, local sources suggest that there has been a boomerang effect on young adults. Allan Burke might be called the eyes, ears and mouth of Emmons County. In 1993, Burke and his wife Leah bought the *Emmons County Record*, the oldest business in the county and the third-largest weekly newspaper in the state. While Burke is semi-retired, he still keeps close tabs on the community as the publisher emeritus.

Before the ag boom hit, "our farmers were aging, and nobody wanted their kids to come back and farm. But now, they want junior to come home ... [and] we have a lot of young couples and young farmers who have come back" to work the land, he said. Burke's son graduated from high school in 2007 and recently moved to Washington state to teach high school biology—a common move for many graduates in the past. "Nobody stayed around here, or very few," said Burke. But that appears to be changing. "Now there's like five or six boys from his class [of about 34] who are farming, and then there's a couple who are in agronomy."

Vold has seen the same phenomenon in Carrington. "There was a point in North Dakota [where we said] goodbye to our kids. Graduation felt like a funeral. It was like, 'Well, nice having you here for these 18 years, and you're all going to go off and get jobs everywhere around the country,'" said Vold. "Now, we have all kinds of people, young families [coming back]. Many of them are farming, but [there are] also a lot of other choices. We have three excellent doctors in our clinic and three physician assistants, and they're all from here."

Vold's middle child, Matthew, "grew up here, went off to college, came back, and he's got a good job" in the business office at the pasta plant in town. Just 26 years old, "he bought a house here in town. Doing better that way than I was" at that age, Vold said.

Though Vold's older son, Bryan, said he enjoys living in the Twin Cities, he hasn't dismissed the idea of coming home. "I definitely have not ruled it out." Bryan Vold is single right now, but if he were raising a family, he said, "I would rather do it in Carrington. It just feels better."

> *"Never again will 18-year-olds*
> *graduate directly from high school to*
> *jobs that pay well enough to buy a*
> *house and support a family."*

The Middle Class Is Gone

Edward McClelland

In the following article, Edward McClelland argues that a major reason for the decline of the middle class is the role of capitalism in concentrating wealth in the ownership class. He claims that a lack of government intervention has resulted in a stagnant economy and higher income inequality. He suggests that the government needs to raise taxes of the wealthy, protect labor unions, and raise the minimum wage. McClelland is a journalist and author of numerous books about workers and the economy.

As you read, consider the following questions:

1. Why does the author consider the prosperous forty years after World War Two a "fluke"?
2. Why does the author believe that more government intervention is needed to stimulate the economy?
3. According to McClelland, what should the government do to provide upward mobility for the lower classes?

"RIP, the middle class: 1946-2013," Edward McClelland, September 20, 2013. Reprinted by permission.

I know I'm dating myself by writing this, but I remember the middle class.

I grew up in an automaking town in the 1970s, when it was still possible for a high school graduate—or even a high school dropout—to get a job on an assembly line and earn more money than a high school teacher.

"I had this student," my history teacher once told me, "a real chucklehead. Just refused to study. Dropped out of school, a year or so later, he came back to see me. He pointed out the window at a brand-new Camaro and said, 'That's my car.' Meanwhile, I was driving a beat-up station wagon. I think he was an electrician's assistant or something. He handed light bulbs to an electrician."

In our neighbors' driveways, in their living rooms, in their backyards, I saw the evidence of prosperity distributed equally among the social classes: speedboats, Corvette Stingrays, waterbeds, snowmobiles, motorcycles, hunting rifles, RVs, CB radios. I've always believed that the '70s are remembered as the Decade That Taste Forgot because they were a time when people without culture or education had the money to not only indulge their passions, but flaunt them in front of the entire nation. It was an era, to use the title of a 1975 sociological study of a Wisconsin tavern, of blue-collar aristocrats.

That all began to change in the 1980s. The recession at the beginning of that decade—America's first Great Recession—was the beginning of the end for the bourgeois proletariat. Steelworkers showed up for first shift to find padlocks on mill gates. Autoworkers were laid off for years. The lucky ones were transferred to plants far from home. The unlucky never built another car.

When I was growing up, it was assumed that America's shared prosperity was the natural endpoint of our economy's development, that capitalism had produced the workers paradise to which Communism unsuccessfully aspired. Now, with the perspective of 40 years, it's obvious that the nonstop economic expansion that lasted from the end of World War II to the Arab oil embargo of 1973 was a historical fluke, made possible by the fact that the

United States was the only country to emerge from that war with its industrial capacity intact. Unfortunately, the middle class—especially the blue-collar middle class—is also starting to look like a fluke, an interlude between Gilded Ages that more closely reflect the way most societies structure themselves economically. For the majority of human history—and in the majority of countries today—there have been only two classes: aristocracy and peasantry. It's an order in which the many toil for subsistence wages to provide luxuries for the few. Twentieth century America temporarily escaped this stratification, but now, as statistics on economic inequality demonstrate, we're slipping back in that direction. Between 1970 and today, the share of the nation's income that went to the middle class—households earning two-thirds to double the national median—fell from 62 percent to 45 percent. Last year, the wealthiest 1 percent took in 19 percent of America's income—their highest share since 1928. It's as though the New Deal and the modern labor movement never happened.

Here's the story of a couple whose working lives began during the Golden Age of middle-class employment, and are ending in this current age of inequality. Gary Galipeau was born in Syracuse, N.Y., in the baby boom sweet spot of 1948. At age 19, he hired in at his hometown's flagship business, the Carrier Corp., which gave Syracuse the title "Air-Conditioning Capital of the World." Starting at $2.37 an hour, Galipeau worked his way into the skilled trades, eventually becoming a metal fabricator earning 10 times his original wage.

"Understand," he said, "in the mid-'60s, you could figuratively roll out of bed and find a manufacturing job."

Voss joined Carrier after dropping out of Syracuse University, and getting laid off from an industrial laundry.

"It was 1978," she said. "You could still go from factory to factory. One day, a friend and I were looking for a job. We saw this big building. We said, 'Must be jobs in there.' In those days, you could fill out an application and get an interview the same day. I was offered a job within three or four days, making window units.

I sprayed glue on fiberglass insulation, stuck it inside units—400 a day, nearly one a minute. I was told, 'After five years, you'll have a job for life. You'll be golden.'"

Galipeau and Voss, who met working at Carrier, lost their jobs in 2004, when the company moved the last of its Syracuse manufacturing operations to Singapore. There, even the most skilled workers were paid half the $27 an hour Galipeau had earned as a metalworker. The corporation they'd expected to spend their careers with divorced them in middle age, and now they had to bridge the years until Social Security and Medicare. Eligible for Trade Adjustment Assistance, because her job had moved overseas, Voss earned a two-year degree in health information technology— "a fancy way of saying medical records."

Even with the degree, Voss couldn't find decent-paying work in healthcare, so she took a job with a sump pump manufacturer, for $12.47 an hour—a substantial drop from Carrier, but decent money for Central New York in the A.D. of A/C. (The No. 1 employer of ex-Carrier workers is an Iroquois casino.) Less than two weeks into the new job, a thread on Voss' work glove wrapped itself around a drill press, taking Voss' finger with it. The digit was torn off at the first knuckle. When Voss returned to work, two months later, she found the factory so distressing that she soon took a medical records job in a hospital, paying $2.50 an hour less.

After earning a degree in human resources management, Galipeau found that 56 was too old to start a new career. Fortunate enough to draw a full pension from Carrier, Galipeau took a part-time job at a supermarket meat counter, for the health insurance. Syracuse's leading vocations are now education and medicine— the training of the young and the preservation of the old. Where nothing is left for the middle-aged, or the middle class, it's difficult to be both.

The shrinking of the middle class is not a failure of capitalism. It's a failure of government. Capitalism has been doing exactly what it was designed to do: concentrating wealth in the ownership class, while providing the mass of workers with just enough wages to feed, house and clothe themselves. Young people who graduate from college to $9.80 an hour jobs as sales clerks or data processors are giving up on the concept of employment as a vehicle for improving their financial fortunes: In a recent survey, 24 percent defined the American dream as "not being in debt." They're not trying to get ahead. They're just trying to get to zero.

That's the natural drift of the relationship between capital and labor, and it can only be arrested by an activist government that chooses to step in as a referee. The organizing victories that founded the modern union movement were made possible by the National Labor Relations Act, a piece of New Deal legislation guaranteeing workers the right to bargain collectively. The plotters of the 1936-37 Flint Sit Down Strike, which gave birth to the United Auto Workers, tried to time their action to coincide with the inauguration of Frank Murphy, Michigan's newly elected New Deal governor. Murphy dispatched the National Guard to Flint, but instead of ordering his guardsmen to throw the workers out of the plants, as he legally could have done, he ordered them to ensure the workers remained safely inside. The strike resulted in a nickel an hour raise and an end to arbitrary firings. It guaranteed the success of the UAW, whose high wages and benefits set the standard for American workers for the next 45 years. (I know a Sit Down Striker who died on Sept. 17, at 98 years old, an age he might not have attained without the lifetime health benefits won by the UAW.)

The United States will never again be as wealthy as it was in the 1950s and '60s. Never again will 18-year-olds graduate directly from high school to jobs that pay well enough to buy a house and support a family. (Even the auto plants now demand a few years in junior college.) That was inevitable, due to the recovery of our World War II enemies, and automation that enables 5,000 workers to build the same number of cars that once required 25,000 hands. What was not inevitable was the federal government withdrawing its supervision of the economy at the precise moment Americans began to need it more than at any time since the Great Depression.

Periodical and Internet Sources Bibliography

The following articles have been selected to supplement the diverse views presented in this chapter.

Chris Arnade, "Who Still Believes in the American Dream? *The Atlantic*, September 23, 2015.

David Azerrad and Rea S. Hederman, Jr., "Defending the Dream: Why Income Inequality Doesn't Threaten Opportunity," The Heritage Foundation, September 13, 2012.

Richard Freeman, Eunice Han, David Madland, and Brendan Duke, "Bargaining for the American Dream," Center for American Progress, September 9, 2015. https://www.americanprogress.org/issues/economy/report/2015/09/09/120558/bargaining-for-the -american-dream.

Dwyer Gunn, "What Happened to the American Dream?" *Pacific Standard*, April 7, 2016.

David Kamp, "Rethinking the American Dream," *Vanity Fair*, April 2009.

Mike Kelly, "Is This the End of the American Dream?" NorthJersey .com., April 3, 2016. http://www.northjersey.com/news/kelly-is -this-the-end-of-the-american-dream-1.1537357.

Cecilia Muñoz and Leon Rodriguez, "Keeping the American Dream Alive," U.S. Department of Homeland Security, December 16, 2015. https://www.dhs.gov/blog/2015/12/16/keeping-american- dream-alive.

The Pew Charitable Trusts, "Pursuing the American Dream: Economic Mobility Across Generations," The Pew Charitable Trusts, 2012.

David Rotman, "Tech Slowdown Threatens the American Dream," *MIT Technology Review*, April 6, 2016.

Andrew Soergel, "Even Americans Can't Afford the American Dream," *U.S. News & World Report,* February 3, 2016.

Jon Talton, "Can Jobs Still Provide a Pathway to the American Dream? *The Seattle Times,* December 30, 2015.

How Can the Wealth Gap Be Addressed?

Chapter Preface

M ost Americans are in agreement that the wealth gap is a serious problem. A 2014 USA Today/Pew Research survey found that two-thirds of those polled believed that the gap between the rich and everyone else had increased in the previous ten years. A majority agreed that inequality was an issue that needed to be addressed immediately.

When talking about the differences between the rich and the poor, economists distinguish between income and wealth. Income is what a wage earner brings home in one year. Wealth is what a household has accumulated over time. One researcher, New York University economist Edward Wolff, found that that while the highest earning families earned almost 60 percent of all income, the richest fifth held almost 90 percent of all wealth. Much of the wealth of low and middle income families includes assets such as houses and retirement savings. That wealth evaporated during the Great Recession when the housing bubble burst and many families lost their homes and jobs.

While there is agreement that the wealth gap is a serious problem, there is debate about what to do about this issue. Most economists do not believe that there is any one solution to the problem of income and wealth inequality. Nor do they agree on the extent of federal involvement in reversing the widening inequality. The importance of the role of government reflects a partisan split. According to a 2014 Pew Research Organization poll, more Democrats than Republicans favor increasing taxes on the wealthy as a way of reducing inequality.

Many economists suggest policies that address the issues of the lower and middle classes. One suggestion is an increase in the minimum wage paid to mostly low-level service jobs. Some economists say that the federal minimum wage should be pegged to the rate of inflation so that low-wage workers won't fall behind as prices rise. Supporting unionization for low and middle wage workers to increase their bargaining power is another proposal that economists say might help maintain a prosperous middle class.

Improving educational opportunities, most experts say, is essential to increasing upward mobility for those in the lower income levels. In many communities, property taxes support local schools. When housing lost value during the Great Recession and banks foreclosed on homes, students at wealthier neighborhood schools maintained their advantages while students in depressed neighborhoods lost needed resources. Many economists say that providing free quality early childhood education, world-class primary and secondary schools for all neighborhoods, and assistance with college or technical schools will allow anyone to make the most of their skills and talents.

Many policy makers look at U.S. tax policies as opportunities to build up the middle class. During some presidential administrations, taxes were cut for the wealthy, assuming that they would expand business and grow the economy. These policies, economists say, didn't always work as intended. Some policy makers advocate increasing taxes on the wealthy to fund education and infrastructure improvements.

The wide variety of opinions on how to address income inequality are reflected in the following viewpoints. Not everyone thinks that something needs to be done. Those that agree that changes in fiscal policies are needed offer different opinions on the role of government and the impact of party politics on economic policies.

> *"The issue of wealth and income
> inequality is the great moral issue
> of our time, it is the great economic
> issue of our time, and it is the great
> political issue of our time."*

Government Should Narrow the Wealth Gap

Bernie Sanders

*In the following article, taken from his 2016 presidential campaign
website, Bernie Sanders expresses his outrage about the wealth that
is owned and controlled by the 1 percent in America. He outlines
his proposed policies for reducing income and wealth inequality and
help the lower and middle classes. Among his policies are raising
estate taxes, increasing the federal minimum wage, and investing
in infrastructure projects. While Sanders's campaign caught fire,
particularly among young voters, he ultimately failed to win the
Democratic nomination. Sanders is a senator from Vermont.*

As you read, consider the following questions:

1. What statistics does Sanders use to support his argument
   that there is large wealth and income inequality in the
   U.S.?
2. What policies does Sanders propose to increase wages
   and employment?
3. What policies does Sanders propose that will support
   children and families?

"Income and Wealth Inequality," Bernie Sanders, 2016.

Today, we live in the richest country in the history of the world, but that reality means little because much of that wealth is controlled by a tiny handful of individuals.

The issue of wealth and income inequality is the great moral issue of our time, it is the great economic issue of our time, and it is the great political issue of our time.

America now has more wealth and income inequality than any major developed country on earth, and the gap between the very rich and everyone else is wider than at any time since the 1920s.

The reality is that since the mid-1980s there has been an enormous transfer of wealth from the middle class and the poor to the wealthiest people in this country. That is the Robin Hood principle in reverse. That is unacceptable and that has got to change.

There is something profoundly wrong when the top one-tenth of one percent owns almost as much wealth as the bottom 90 percent.

> "Just as the commandment 'Thou shalt not kill' sets a clear limit in order to safeguard the value of human life, today we also have to say 'thou shalt not' to an economy of exclusion and inequality. Such an economy kills. How can it be that it is not a news item when an elderly homeless person dies of exposure, but it is news when the stock market loses two points?"
>
> —Pope Francis

There is something profoundly wrong when 58 percent of all new income since the Wall Street crash has gone to the top one percent.

Despite huge advancements in technology and productivity, millions of Americans are working longer hours for lower wages. The real median income of male workers is $783 less than it was 42 years ago; while the real median income of female workers is over $1,300 less than it was in 2007. That is unacceptable and that has got to change.

There is something profoundly wrong when we have a proliferation of millionaires and billionaires at the same time as millions of Americans work longer hours for lower wages and we have the highest childhood poverty rate of nearly any developed country on earth.

There is something profoundly wrong when one family owns more wealth than the bottom 130 million Americans.

The reality is that for the past 40 years, Wall Street and the billionaire class has rigged the rules to redistribute wealth and income to the wealthiest and most powerful people of this country.

This campaign is sending a message to the billionaire class: "you can't have it all." You can't get huge tax breaks while children in this country go hungry. You can't continue sending our jobs to China while millions are looking for work. You can't hide your profits in the Cayman Islands and other tax havens, while there are massive unmet needs on every corner of this nation. Your greed has got to end. You cannot take advantage of all the benefits of America, if you refuse to accept your responsibilities as Americans.

As president, Senator Bernie Sanders will reduce income and wealth inequality by:

1. Demanding that the wealthy and large corporations pay their fair share in taxes. As president, Sen. Sanders will stop corporations from shifting their profits and jobs overseas to avoid paying U.S. income taxes. He will create a progressive estate tax on the top 0.3 percent of Americans who inherit more than $3.5 million. He will also enact a tax on Wall Street speculators who caused millions of Americans to lose their jobs, homes, and life savings.

2. Increasing the federal minimum wage from $7.25 to $15 an hour by 2020. In the year 2015, no one who works 40 hours a week should be living in poverty.

3. Putting at least 13 million Americans to work by investing $1 trillion over five years towards rebuilding our crumbling roads, bridges, railways, airports, public transit systems, ports, dams, wastewater plants, and other infrastructure needs.

4. Reversing trade policies like NAFTA, CAFTA, and PNTR with China that have driven down wages and caused the loss of millions of jobs. If corporate America wants us to buy their products they need to manufacture those products in this country, not in China or other low-wage countries.

5. Creating 1 million jobs for disadvantaged young Americans by investing $5.5 billion in a youth jobs program. Today, the youth unemployment rate is off the charts. We have got to end this tragedy by making sure teenagers and young adults have the jobs they need to move up the economic ladder.

6. Fighting for pay equity by signing the Paycheck Fairness Act into law. It is an outrage that women earn just 78 cents for every dollar a man earns.

7. Making tuition free at public colleges and universities throughout America. Everyone in this country who studies hard should be able to go to college regardless of income.

8. Expanding Social Security by lifting the cap on taxable income above $250,000. At a time when the senior poverty rate is going up, we have got to make sure that every American can retire with dignity and respect.

9. Guaranteeing healthcare as a right of citizenship by enacting a Medicare for all single-payer healthcare system. It's time for the U.S. to join every major industrialized country on earth and provide universal healthcare to all.

10. Requiring employers to provide at least 12 weeks of paid family and medical leave; two weeks of paid vacation; and 7 days of paid sick days. Real family values are about making sure that parents have the time they need to bond with their babies and take care of their children and relatives when they get ill.

11. Enacting a universal childcare and prekindergarten program. Every psychologist understands that the most formative years for a human being is from the ages 0-3. We have got to make sure every family in America has the opportunity to send their kids to a high quality childcare and pre-K program.

12. Making it easier for workers to join unions by fighting for the Employee Free Choice Act. One of the most significant reasons for the 40-year decline in the middle class is that the rights of workers to collectively bargain for better wages and benefits have been severely undermined.

13. Breaking up huge financial institutions so that they are no longer too big to fail. Seven years ago, the taxpayers of this country bailed out Wall Street because they were too big to fail. Yet, 3 out of the 4 largest financial institutions are 80 percent bigger today than before we bailed them out. Sen. Sanders has introduced legislation to break these banks up. As president, he will fight to sign this legislation into law.

> "*A significant redistribution of wealth to the poorer part of the population might, by improving nutrition and family stability, generate increased upward mobility.*"

Tax the Rich to Invest in the Poor

Gary Becker and Richard Posner

In the following viewpoint, Gary Becker and Richard Posner argue that wealthy people tend to secure their wealth across generations. They invest their resources into their children to guarantee their health, education, and success. The authors claim that taxing the richest 1 percent of people to invest into the poor might increase the upward mobility of those at the lowest levels of wealth and income. Becker was a Nobel Prize–winning economist and a professor of economics and sociology at the University of Chicago. Posner is a judge on the United States Court of Appeals for the Seventh Circuit and a senior lecturer at the University of Chicago Law School.

As you read, consider the following questions:

1. How is the geography of the U.S. related to social mobility?
2. According to the authors, why has social mobility remained stagnant while income inequality increased?
3. Why do the authors recommend that the government enact policies to increase social mobility?

"Social Mobility and Income Inequality," Posner, February 2, 2014. Reprinted by permission.

A s Becker notes, recent research indicates that social mobility (how much a person rises or falls in the income distribution relative to his or her parents) in the United States has remained constant, albeit at a low level by comparison with other wealthy countries (for a partial summary of this research, see Raj Chetty et al., "The Equality of Opportunity Project," www.equality-of -opportunity.org) at the same time that inequality of income in the United States has risen, and now far exceeds that in the other wealthy countries.

A striking finding by the researchers is the high geographical variance in mobility. The probability that a person whose parents were in the bottom fifth of the income distribution will rise to the top fifth is roughly twice that for persons living in the northeast or on the west coast than for persons living in the south and the midwest—about 10 percent versus 5 percent. This is probably related to the pattern of immigration, the quality of schools, and the fact that educated and ambitious people tend to find the northeast and far west culturally more congenial than the south, the border states, and the midwest, with their religiosity, conservatism, gun mania, Confederate nostalgia, higher crime rates, and greater poverty.

The fact that mobility has not declined during a period in which inequality of incomes has grown may seem paradoxical, but is not. Imagine that all incomes were close to being equal. Then social mobility would be close to zero because there would be so little to gain from getting a better job or working harder. And by the same token social mobility might be very great in a society yet income inequality also be very great. For suppose that whether one had a high or a low income was almost entirely a matter of luck. Then the children of rich and of poor families would be quite likely to changes places in the income distribution, regardless of how skewed that distribution was.

But while social mobility and income inequality can thus move together, I am surprised that social mobility does not decrease as income inequality rises. The wealthier a family is, the more likely its children are to be secure against dropping significantly below their parents' rank in the income distribution. One reason is that wealthy people (unless they are sports or entertainment figures) are apt to have high IQs, especially now that, with the decline of discrimination, there is more assortative mating than there used to be. Another reason is that the children of wealthy people have a better shot at admission to the best schools and colleges. This is partly because the kids tend to be smart, partly because the parents provide positive role models for the children and also can invest heavily in tutoring and other aids to their children's education, and partly because colleges and universities tend to favor the admission of rich kids, who can be expected to become generous donors. And finally the children of the rich receive excellent nutrition and medical care, hence tend to be healthier than the average child.

One reason social mobility seems not to have been significantly affected by the rising inequality of income in the United States is that much of the growth in inequality is a result of increased incomes of the wealthiest 1 percent of the population, whose share of national income has grown from 13 percent in 1982 to 22 percent today, and whose after-tax income has increased almost threefold in that period. Even if one percent of the population can immunize itself from downward mobility, overall mobility should not be greatly affected. This is so even though if the top 1 percent have become richer, the bottom 99 percent have become poorer. But becoming poorer needn't make a person likelier to climb out of poverty, since the poorer one is, the harder the climb.

There are several reasons for encouraging social mobility, and this should make us resist complacency about the fact that it hasn't changed much despite the increased inequality of incomes, and focus rather on the fact that it's much lower than in our peer countries. One reason for trying to increase mobility is to stimulate ambition and effort. If people born into families who are low on the income distribution sense few opportunities to rise, they will have little incentive to try to better their lot. A related reason is that many highly successful people had humble beginnings; and we would

THE REALITY OF INCOME INEQUALITY

Americans are bothered by the increasingly unequal distribution of wealth in the U.S., according to several surveys. Interestingly, studies also show that most Americans have a poor understanding of how unevenly wealth is distributed, according to a 2011 study by economists Michael Norton and Dan Ariely.

A viral video, published in 2012 and based on their study, highlighted substantial differences between Americans' perceptions of income distribution and the reality. The video showed in graphic form how Americans think wealth is distributed: The average American believes that the wealthiest fifth own 59 percent of the wealth and that the bottom 40 percent own 9 percent. The reality is strikingly different. The top 20 percent of US households own more than 84 percent of the wealth, and the bottom 40 percent combine for a paltry 0.3 percent.

like our educational and social welfare systems to discover and assist and encourage these people when young. A further reason for trying to increase mobility is to discourage people from seeking betterment of their lot through crime or gambling, activities that can be attractive to people who despair of improving their lot by lawful work rather than crime and by effort rather than luck.

And finally, although the fact that social mobility has not fallen as income inequality has risen may seem to imply that reducing inequality would not increase mobility, that may not be correct. Social mobility may not have fallen, I have suggested, only because the rise in inequality has been so skewed in favor of a small fraction of the population. A significant redistribution of wealth to the poorer part of the population might, by improving nutrition and family stability, generate increased upward mobility.

> *"Taxing the rich doesn't put money in the hands of the poor, it puts it in the hands of the government, who then transfers it to any one of a number of politically favored groups."*

Higher Taxes on the Rich Won't Reduce Income Inequality

Doug Mataconis

In the following viewpoint, Doug Mataconis argues that imposing higher taxes on wealthy people will not alleviate income inequality. He contends that transferring wealth from the top 1 percent to the government to distribute often just supports failing institutions. Instead, he proposes reforming government and tax policies to encourage upward mobility. Mataconis is a blogger on the site Outside the Beltway.

As you read, consider the following questions:

1. According to Mataconis, what is the effect of imposing higher taxes on wealthy people?
2. What does the author think will be the impact of the retirement of Baby Boomers?
3. What does the author propose as a solution to the problem of lack of upward mobility?

Source: "Taxing The Rich Won't Alleviate Income Inequality," Doug Mataconis, from Outside the Beltway, October 30, 2011.

The two themes that seem to be coming out of the pundits who are sympathetic to the Occupy movement (as opposed to the movement itself, which remains a befuddled miasma of causes with no coherent message) are the twin ideas of income inequality and increasing the taxes on the "rich," as we saw in things like the so-called Buffett Rule which President Obama proposed in September, but never really bothered to turn into a concrete proposal. Accepting for the sake of argument that these are both legitimate issues, Ross Douthat reminds us this morning that taxing the rich, whatever merits it might have with respect to fiscal policy won't do anything about income inequality:

> From the drum circles of Zuccotti Park to the hustings of Barack Obama's re-election push, a suddenly invigorated liberalism thinks that it has the answer to this angst: a renewed demand for higher taxes on America's richest 1 percent. And if all you care about is reducing measured income inequality, then the Occupy Wall Streeters and their Democratic admirers have it right. Tax millionaires sufficiently and you'll end up with a more equal society. The tallest poppies will be trimmed, and some of their income will find its way to someone's else pocket.
>
> But true social mobility and broadly shared prosperity are not so easily achieved. Remember that those tax dollars, once collected, would not be disbursed with perfect effectiveness to the most deserving members of the American middle class. Instead, they would be used to buy a little more time for our failing public institutions—postponing a reckoning with unsustainable pension commitments, delaying necessary reforms in our entitlement system and propping up an educational sector whose results don't match the costs.
>
> More spending in these areas won't necessarily buy us more mobility. The public-sector workplace has become a kind of artificial Eden, whose fortunate inhabitants enjoy solid pay and 1950s-style job security and retirement benefits, all of it paid for by their less-fortunate private-sector peers. Some on the left have convinced themselves that this "success" can lay the foundation for a broader middle-class revival. But if a bloated public sector

were the blueprint for a thriving middle-class society, then the whole world would be beating a path to Greece's door.

Our entitlement system, meanwhile, is designed to redistribute wealth. But this redistribution doesn't go from the idle rich to the working poor; it goes from young to old, working-age savings to retiree consumption, middle-class parents to empty-nest seniors. The Congressional Budget Office's new report on income inequality points out that growing Medicare costs are part of the reason upper-income retirees receive a larger share of federal spending than they did 30 years ago, while working-age households with children receive "a much smaller and declining share of transfers." Absent reforms, this mismatch will only grow more pronounced: by the 2030s, Medicare recipients will receive $3 in benefits for every dollar they paid in.

Then there's the public education system, theoretically the nation's most important socioeconomic equalizer. Yet even though government spending on K-to-12 education has more than doubled since the 1970s, test scores have flatlined and the United States has fallen behind its developed-world rivals. Meanwhile, federal spending on higher education has been undercut by steadily inflating tuitions, in what increasingly looks like an academic answer to the housing bubble. (If the Occupy Wall Street dream of student loan forgiveness were fulfilled, this cycle would probably just continue.)

Douthat is largely correct here. There may be perfectly good reasons to increase taxes on higher income earners that relate to the Federal Budget deficit. Additionally, as I've said here other times, the idea that tax increases should be ruled off-the-table in negotiations over a debt deal is as absurd of an idea as the idea that defense spending or entitlements should be off the table. If we're going to get our fiscal house in order, and we need to if we want to avoid the problems that Europe is facing now at some point in our own future, then we need to have everything on the table, including comprehensive tax reform that is likely to mean that higher income earners pay more even if their rates go down.

That's not ideology, it's political reality and plain old common sense because politically we're never going to be able to bring the budget under control with only spending cuts or only tax increases, it's going to take a combination of the two.

What makes for smart fiscal policy, though, doesn't necessarily do anything to deal with income inequality, or the lack of mobility that the economy has experienced in recent years. As Douthat notes, taxing the rich doesn't put money in the hands of the poor, it puts in the hands of the government, who then transfers it to any one of a number of politically favored groups. Right now, the biggest government-controlled wealth transfers go from the relatively poor young to the typically better-off retired, and that's a phenomenon that's only going to accelerate as the Baby Boomers retire. If anything, that is going increase income inequality regardless of what we do about taxes on the "rich."

Moreover, it's simply a lie that taxing the rich is going to do anything to help the poor in the long run. It's a lie built on simplistic notions of egalitarianism, the notion that people who have succeeded have done so nefariously, and the idea that there's just something wrong with being "too rich," whatever that means. It works politically for the same reason that populism and appeals to envy have always worked, and it's totally wrong. The government can't make people equal. In fact, if the Occupy Wall Street crowd were paying attention, they'd realize that it's government manipulation of the economy that has created the very inequality they complain of. And yet, they have the illusion that the solution to their perceived problems is more, and bigger, government.

Douthat suggests an alternative:

> The alternative to this liberalism should not, however, be the kind of reverse class warfare currently being championed by the not-Romney candidates in the Republican field, whose flat-tax fantasies would ask working Americans to bear more of the burden for public institutions that have been failing them for years.

Rather, it should be a kind of small-government egalitarianism, which would seek to reform the government before we pour more money into it, along lines that encourage upward mobility and benefit the middle class. This would mean seeking a carefully means-tested welfare state, a less special interest-friendly tax code, and a public sector that worked for taxpayers and parents rather than the other way around.

The devil, as always, is in the details but, considering that what we've been doing for the last 40 years or so clearly isn't working perhaps it's worth looking into.

> "*In a similar vein, a recent Oxfam study found that the richest 85 people in the world own the same amount of wealth as the bottom half of the world's population.*"

Redistribution Is the Answer

David Lipton

In the following viewpoint, David Lipton argues that well-designed government policies to redistribute income can reduce income inequality. He suggests that income taxes that are progressive work better than flat taxes. He finds that increasing expenditures on health and education, especially post-secondary education, can increase social mobility. He proposes that countries provide pensions for retired workers to prevent old-age poverty. This is an excerpt from a speech presented at the Peterson Institute for International Economics in Washington, DC. Lipton is the first deputy managing director of the International Monetary Fund.

As you read, consider the following questions:

1. What does the author mean by the term "redistribution policy"?
2. What is the Gini coefficient?
3. What nationwide expenditures does the author think will improve economic opportunities for the poor?

"Fiscal Policy and Income Inequality," David Lipton, March 13, 2014. Reprinted by permission.

Thank you for providing me the opportunity to present the key findings of a new IMF study on fiscal policy and income inequality.

Income inequality has been rising in many parts of the world in recent decades. This, and the social tensions associated with fiscal consolidation that many have faced in part stemming from the global financial crisis, have put the distributional impact of governments' tax and spending policies at the heart of the public debate in many countries. Of course, the question of just how much redistribution the state should do is, at its core, a political one that economic analysis cannot answer. But I think that we can all agree that whatever degree of redistribution governments choose, it should be done with fiscal instruments that achieve their distributional objectives at a minimum cost to economic efficiency.

The design of these growth-friendly, efficient redistributive fiscal policies is the focus of my presentation today.

Some may be surprised that the Fund is engaging in this debate on the design of redistributive policies. The truth of the matter is that we have been at this for a long time. Assessing the effect of tax and expenditure policies on efficiency, and any potential tradeoffs with distributional goals, has long been an important component of the IMF's policy advice. Furthermore, the design of Fund-supported programs is inevitably influenced by the authorities' distributional objectives. Whenever we discuss social safety net programs, or the level of health and education expenditures, and how to generate the revenues or finance to sustain them, subjects we routinely address, we are discussing redistribution policy.

Our record for protecting the poor in the design of Fund-supported programs has a longstanding history, going back to the Camdessus era in the 1980s.

So, this paper should thus be seen as the Fund's advice to its membership, based on our extensive experience. Of course, one reason why we are discussing this issue today is that the interest in redistribution as reflected in public surveys and our discussions with our members is higher than in the past. Our members want to explore with us how they can pursue distributive policies in an efficient manner.

The key message that I want to convey today is that when it comes to fiscal redistribution, design matters. This is consistent with a recent IMF staff study by Ostry et al, which finds that, on average, inequality is associated with lower growth. Thus fiscal redistribution can help support growth because it reduces inequality. What we see is a diversity of experience across countries with redistributive policies. Some redistributive fiscal policies can help improve efficiency and support growth, such as those that enhance the human capital of low-income households. Let me be clear, redistributive policies can generate a tradeoff between equality and efficiency, and if misconceived, this tradeoff can be very costly. I will cite examples of this problem later on. But as I said, design matters, and smart design can help to minimize the adverse effects of redistributive policies on incentives to work, save, and invest.

My presentation today will cover three broad topics, including trends in inequality, the experience of countries in using redistributive policy, and options for achieving more efficient redistribution.

Let us first move to the discussion of trends in inequality. This figure presents the trends in the average Gini coefficient for disposable income. Gini coefficient ranges from 0 to 1, with larger values representing higher inequality. Disposable income is market income after income and wealth taxes and cash transfers. Over the last three decades, the Gini coefficient has increased in most countries, indicating an increase in inequality. In Latin America and sub-Saharan Africa, however, there has been a declining level of inequality more recently. What is most striking in the figure, however, are the persistent differences across regions, with Latin America having the highest inequality and the advanced economies having the lowest.

More recently, there has been great attention to the rising share of top income earners. The trends across countries appear mixed.

In some economies, such as the United States and South Africa, the share of the top one-percent has increased dramatically in recent decades, but not so in continental Europe and Japan, where it has been largely unchanged. There are differing views of the causes of the rising share of the top one percent. Some emphasize the impact of globalization and new technologies, while others highlight policy choices, such as reductions in tax rates, and others the rent-seeking behavior of executives.

If we compare the distribution of income with that of wealth, we can see that wealth is much more unequally distributed, as indicated by the higher Gini coefficients. In a similar vein, a recent Oxfam study found that the richest 85 people in the world own the same amount of wealth as the bottom half of the world's population. Both the high degree of inequality of wealth, and the increased share of the top one percent, have fueled the recent debate on income and wealth taxation.

Let us now turn to country experience with different instruments for fiscal redistribution. We will start with the advanced economies, where countries are already doing a substantial amount of redistribution. The average market income Gini, i.e., in the absence of any fiscal redistribution, is 0.43. Redistributive transfers and taxes reduce inequality by about a third, with about two-thirds of this coming from transfers.

[This] does not include the impact of in-kind benefits, such as public spending on health, education, and housing. In the countries selected here, it is estimated that in-kind transfers further reduce the market Gini, on average, by more than 10 percent. Thus, we can conclude that based on both direct and in-kind benefits, fiscal policy has played a major role in reducing inequality in advanced economies, although its extent varies across countries.

So what about developing economies? Developing economies here include both emerging and low-income countries. It appears that fiscal policy has played a much more modest role there. Let's first look at the tax side. The levels of tax revenues are significantly lower in developing economies, with the exception of emerging

Europe. In terms of composition, indirect taxes, like the VAT, account for a much larger share, which tend to be less progressive than direct taxes such as the income tax. On the expenditure side, again, levels of redistributive expenditures are much lower, particularly when it comes to social protection.

A lot of the social spending in developing economies is not well designed and targeted and actually increases inequality. With the exception of emerging Europe, the poorest 40 percent of the population receive less than 20 percent of the benefits of social protection spending. The coverage of social benefits, in terms of the percentage of poor households that receive benefits, is also low, except in emerging Europe and Latin America.

In this context, it is also important to note that many developing countries use energy subsidies as a form of social assistance. But as we underscored in the work we presented at the Peterson Institute last year, these subsidies disproportionately benefit upper-income groups.

Education and health spending in developing economies is also not well targeted and exacerbates inequality. In many developing economies, for example, the poorest 40 percent receive less than 40 percent of the total benefits, which contributes to inequality of opportunity and low intergenerational mobility. One reason for this is that the poor often lack access to these services, reflecting the fact that many of them live in poor rural areas while services are concentrated in urban areas.

This discussion of the redistributive effect of fiscal policy in advanced and developing economies has important implications for the design of fiscal consolidation packages. As shown in our paper, a number of economies have adopted progressive adjustment measures during their recent fiscal consolidations. As a result, the burden of these adjustment measures on the bottom 20 percent of the population was lower than that of upper income groups. For example, in Greece, Latvia, Portugal, Romania, and Spain, cuts in public sector pay had a smaller effect on civil servants toward the bottom of the pay-scale. In Spain and the United

Kingdom, increases in income taxation were born more heavily by upper-income groups.

Let us now turn to options for designing fiscal redistribution in an efficient manner. We see four key considerations in designing efficient redistributive fiscal policy:

First, redistributive fiscal policy should be consistent with macroeconomic policy objectives. The level of spending on redistribution, for example, should be consistent with macroeconomic stability. In addition, the benefits of additional spending on redistribution should be compared with the benefits of raising spending in other priority areas, such as infrastructure.

Second, taxes and expenditures should be evaluated jointly. For example, an increase in VAT revenues, used to finance higher spending in secondary education, could—on net—be progressive.

Third, the design of redistribution policies should account for both redistributive and efficiency objectives. Some redistributive policies may in fact enhance efficiency, such as those that strengthen human capital. But with others there may be the need to manage a tradeoff.

And fourth, design should take into account administrative capacity.

Based on these principles, we examine a range of options for achieving redistribution efficiently. The paper provides an extensive discussion of instruments. In the interest of time, I will focus on a few of the most important options discussed in the paper. These measures could be implemented as part of long-term fiscal reforms aimed at achieving redistributive objectives more efficiently. They could also be integrated into the design of fiscal consolidation strategies that aim to help governments achieve redistributive goals at a lower fiscal cost.

The primary contribution of taxation to reducing income inequality is through its financing of redistributive spending measures in a way that it does not harm growth. Nevertheless, taxes can also have a direct effect on redistribution. This is particularly the case for income taxes.

To start, countries could consider making their income tax systems more progressive. For example, in economies where a flat rate is used, there may be scope for more tax progression at the top. Since the mid 1990s, 27 countries—especially in Central and Eastern Europe and Central Asia—have introduced flat tax systems, usually with a low marginal rate. The top personal income tax rate must, however, be set with care. If it is too high, taxpayers will find ways to avoid or evade the tax and a higher rate may no longer raise extra revenue. In many developing economies, both fairness and equity could be enhanced by bringing more informal operators into the personal income tax.

There is also scope to more fully utilize property taxes, both as a source of revenue and as an efficient redistributive instrument. This applies also to developing economies, where only Colombia, Namibia, Russia, South Africa, and Uruguay collect more than 1 percent of GDP through recurrent property taxes.

Indirect taxes, including the VAT, are generally less effective in achieving redistributive goals than direct taxes. On the VAT, the recommendation is thus to minimize exemptions and special rates, in order to efficiently raise revenues to help finance pro-poor spending. For instance, elimination of reduced VAT rates in the United Kingdom, and using the proceeds to increase social benefits, would significantly reduce inequality. Earlier work at the IMF has shown that in Ethiopia, the net impact of a uniform VAT, with the proceeds used for general spending on education and health, would have a strong progressive impact. However, where capacity constraints prevent spending programs from reaching the poor, there can be a case for some differentiation in VAT rates, for example for basic foods that are a large part of the spending of the poor.

On the expenditure side, I would like to start first with education. Improving the access of low-income families to education is an efficient tool for boosting equality of opportunity, and over the long run, it can also reduce income inequality. In advanced economies, this entails increasing the access to tertiary education for low-income families, including through scholarships and loans. For developing economies, a strengthening of access to quality secondary education is also required, for example, by eliminating tuition fees.

Along the same lines, improving the access of the poor to health care services in developing economies can provide a head start to greater opportunity and do so in an efficient manner. Some countries, including China, Ghana, India, and Mexico, have taken important steps toward universal coverage in recent years. In advanced economies, maintaining the access of the poor to health services during periods of expenditure constraint is also consistent with efficient redistribution.

To make social transfers more efficient in advanced economies, there could be greater use of active labor market programs and in-work benefits for social benefit recipients. This would, for example, require beneficiaries to participate in active labor market programs, such as job training, as a condition for receiving benefits, as done in Belgium, the Slovak Republic, and Slovenia.

The second reform measure that I will focus on is to expand conditional cash transfer programs in developing economies. These programs make benefits conditional on the attendance of children at health clinics and at school. Means-testing helps keep the fiscal cost low. This policy can help boost both equality of opportunity and income inequality. For instance, the direct impact of such transfers in Brazil and Mexico accounts for one-fifth of the reduction in inequality between 1995 and 2004 in these two countries. A strengthening of administrative capacity, however, is required for implementing these programs in many developing economies.

Pensions have played an important role in reducing income inequality. To improve the sustainability of pension systems and maintain their role in protecting the elderly poor, many economies could consider increasing effective retirement ages. This would need to be accompanied by measures to ensure that lower-income workers are fully protected, as needed, with disability pensions and social assistance if they are unable to work. In developing economies, to ensure wider coverage of pensions at a reasonable fiscal cost, a viable option is to expand noncontributory, means-tested social pensions. Social pensions in some form exist in both emerging and low-income developing countries, including in Chile, Ethiopia, India, and South Africa.

Many countries have been grappling with the twin challenge of putting their pension systems on sound financial footing while safeguarding or expanding their important role in alleviating old-age poverty. I would like to take this opportunity to bring your attention to a new IMF book, "Equitable and Sustainable Pensions: Challenges and Experience," which we are also launching today. The book examines the complex equity issues involved in designing pension systems, including generational and gender equity. It also presents 12 country cases studies to help draw lessons for designing sustainable and equitable pension systems.

Let me end where I started. Many advanced and developing economies are facing the challenge of rising inequality. Fiscal policy has played a major role in reducing inequality in the past and is the primary tool available for governments to affect income distribution. Whether these policies help, or hurt growth, is all a matter of design. And the details matter. Thus, debates on the impact of the government's redistributive policies must go far beyond a mere discussion of tax and spending ratios. In the end, it is design that matters. And on this, the good news is that quite a lot is now known about how governments can best address the challenges of squaring their equity and efficiency concerns, a task on which the Fund stands ready to help.

Thank you.

> "*These results indicate that basic income grants can not only alleviate poverty in purely economic terms, but may also jolt the poor out of the poverty cycle, helping them find work, start their own businesses, and attend school.*"

A Universal Basic Income Would Change the Economy

Scott Santens

In the following viewpoint, Scott Santens proposes that every American be assured of a universal basic income (UBI) of $12,000 per year for citizens over age eighteen, and $4,000 for children. Although this is quite a radical idea in the United States, Santens contends that eliminating wasteful welfare programs and revising the nation's tax policies can make a UBI affordable. He claims that a UBI would allow workers to be more productive, creative, and healthy. Santens is a writer and basic income advocate.

"Why Should We Support the Idea of Universal Basic Income?" Scott Santens, June 26, 2015. Reprinted by permission.

As you read, consider the following questions:

1. Why does Santens claim that capitalism would work better if everyone were guaranteed a basic income?
2. According to Santens, how will a UBI contribute to the circulation of money instead of it pooling at the top 1 percent?
3. How does Santens propose to provide the resources for a universal basic income?

What Would You Do?

So what exactly would you do, if you were guaranteed $1,000 per month for the rest of your life? And yes, that's around what the amount would most likely be here in the United States, at least at first. So think about that amount for a moment, and don't think about what others might do with it, think about what you would do with it. Perhaps you would do more of what you enjoy. So what is that?

Didn't They Try This in Russia?

You've compared this idea to communism, so let's focus on that first. In doing so, let's also talk about what was actually done in the former Soviet Union and not what was intended. What they actually did there, simply put, was transfer the means of production from those who ran the businesses based on market forces, into the hands of a bureaucracy who made decisions based not on market forces but on politics and cronyism. This is a terrible idea. But why is this a terrible idea?

The market works because it is a means of figuring out what people want, the degree to which they want it, and the means of getting it to them. Let's take bread as an example. In Russia, they thought everyone should have bread. That was a decision made by those in power, and they then tried to make that happen, whether everyone wanted bread or not. This did not work so well, and there were shortages. Plus, those with the connections got more than enough while others got none. Trying to give bread to everyone, although noble in gesture, was a failure.

The Magic of Markets

So how do we do it here in America right now? The makers of bread make bread, and sell it to stores, so that people with the money to buy bread, can buy bread. If bread isn't getting bought, less bread is made. If all the bread is getting bought, more bread is made. Those who make the bread aren't making a top-down decision on how much bread to make. They are listening to market forces, and the decision is bottom-up. This is perfect, right? Just the right amount of bread is getting made and at just the right price. No, it's not. Why? And how can this be improved?

Right now only those with the means to pay for bread have a voice for bread. We love to use the term, "voting with our dollars." So is the outcome of that daily election accurate? Does everyone have a voice for bread? No, they don't. There are people with no voice, because they have no dollars. The only way to make sure the market is working as efficiently and effectively as possible to determine what should be getting made, how much to make of it, and where to distribute it, is to make sure everyone has at the very minimum, the means to vote for bread. If they have that money and don't buy bread, there's no need to make and distribute that bread. If the bread is bought, that shows people actually want that bread. So how do we accomplish this improvement of capitalistic markets?

With Universal Basic Income (UBI)

By guaranteeing everyone has at the very least, the minimum amount of voice with which to speak in the marketplace for basic goods and services, we can make sure that the basics needs of life—those specific and universally important to all goods and services like food and shelter—are being created and distributed more efficiently. It makes no sense to make sure 100% of the population gets exactly the same amount of bread. Some may want more than others, and some may want less. It also doesn't make

AMERICA'S ECONOMIC SYSTEM IS UNFAIR

A substantial majority of Americans—65%—say the economic system in this country "unfairly favors powerful interests." Fewer than half as many (31%) say the system "is generally fair to most Americans."

There are notable differences on this issue between—and within—both political parties. Overall, Democrats and Democratic-leaning independents are more likely than Republicans and Republican leaners to view the economic system as unfair (73% vs. 54%).

The ideological gap is even starker. Conservative Republicans are split over the fairness of the economic system: 50% say the system favors the powerful, while just about as many (47%) say it's fair. By contrast, fully 82% of liberal Democrats say the economic system in this country favors powerful interests. A slim 15% think it's fair to most.

"Most Americans say U.S. economic system is unfair, but high-income Republicans disagree," Hannah Fingerhut, February 10, 2016.

sense to only make bread for 70% of the population, thinking that is the true demand for bread, when actually 80% of the population wants it, but 10% have zero means to voice their demand in the market. Bread makers would happily sell more bread and bread eaters would happily buy more bread. It's a win-win to more accurately determine just the right amount.

And that's basic income. It's a win-win for the market and those who comprise the market. It's a way to improve on capitalism and even democracy, by making sure everyone has the minimum amount of *voice*.

Can We Really Improve Capitalism or Is This Just Theory?

If you want actual evidence of how much better capitalism would work with basic income, look at the pilot project in Namibia:

> The village school reported higher attendance rates and that the children were better fed and more attentive. Police statistics showed a 36.5% drop in crime since the introduction of the grants. Poverty rates declined from 86% to 68% (97% to 43% when controlled for migration). Unemployment dropped as well, from 60% to 45%, and there was a 29% increase in average earned income, excluding the basic income grant. These results indicate that basic income grants can not only alleviate poverty in purely economic terms, but may also jolt the poor out of the poverty cycle, helping them find work, start their own businesses, and attend school.

Think about that for a second. Crime plummeted and people given a basic income actually created their own jobs and actually ended up with even greater earnings as a result.

Or how about this psychology experiment as evidence for increased productivity?

> The participants given a choice between either two or three puzzles each spent about 5 minutes working on the puzzle they selected. But those who were also given the option not to participate spent about 7 minutes working on their selected puzzle. Explicitly choosing to do something rather than not to do it greatly increased the amount of time people spent on the task.

This suggests that if we create the option for people to be able to choose not to work, genuinely choosing to work may result in even greater commitment, because it is suddenly a matter of choice and not force. Choice is a powerful motivator.

Speaking of motivation, what does the science have to say about money as an effective motivator for complex and creative tasks?

Larger Rewards Lead to Poorer Performance.

> This is one of the most robust findings in social science, and also one of the most ignored. I spent the last couple of years looking at the science of human motivation, particularly the dynamics of extrinsic motivators and intrinsic motivators. And I'm telling you, it's not even close. If you look at the science, there is a mismatch between what science knows and what business does... That's actually fine for many kinds of 20th century tasks. But for 21st century tasks, that mechanistic, reward-and-punishment approach doesn't work, often doesn't work, and often does harm."

> —Dan Pink

In the 21st century, as we continue quickly automating away half our jobs in the next 20 years—jobs less cognitively-complex and more physically-laborious—we need to enable ourselves to freely pursue our more creative and complex ventures. Some of the best work happening right now, is the stuff being done in our free time—that is unpaid—like Wikipedia and our many other open-source community creations, not to mention all the care work performed for our young and elderly. Basic income is a means of recognizing this unpaid work as having great societal value, and further enabling it.

Or how about the multiplier effect as evidence of enhanced capitalism?

> All those dollars low-wage workers spend create an economic ripple effect. Every extra dollar going into the pockets of low-wage workers, standard economic multiplier models tell us, adds about $1.21 to the national economy. Every extra dollar going into the pockets of a high-income American, by contrast, only adds about 39 cents to the GDP.

This means that by redirecting that money pooling at the top doing comparatively very little, accumulating in ever increasing amounts through continual redistribution upwards from the bottom and middle of the income spectrum, and recirculating that clotted money back down to the bottom and middle, this would actually expand the entire economy while making it more sustainable and more inclusive. This is how the body works. This is how engines work. This is how systems work.

A system cannot exist in perpetuity that is designed for one-way flow. Thomas Piketty demonstrated in his sweeping *Capital in the 21st Century* that perhaps our current system is exactly that—one way. It is up to us to create a true circulatory system for the engine of capitalism. Without monetary circulation, the system as a whole will come to a grinding halt. If Piketty is right, then holding on to an ideology of income and wealth redistribution as "theft" may just be like a heart refusing to pump blood anywhere but the brain.

Capitalism 2.0 Sounds Great and All but Can We Afford It?

Basic income is entirely affordable given all the current and hugely wasteful means-tested programs full of unnecessary bureaucracy that can be consolidated into it. And the cost also depends greatly on the chosen plan. A plan of $12,000 per U.S. citizen over 18, and $4,000 per citizen under 18 amounts to a revenue need of $2.98 trillion, which after all the programs that can be eliminated are rolled into it, requires an additional need of $1.5 trillion or so. So where do we come up with an additional $1.5 trillion?

- A land value tax has been estimated to be a source of revenue of about $1.7 trillion.
- A flat tax of around 40% would be sufficient. Due to the way such a tax works in combination with UBI, this would effectively be a reduction in taxes for about 80% of the population.
- A 10% value added tax (VAT) has been estimated to be a source of revenue of about $750 billion. That could be increased to reach $1.5 trillion or added to other sources of additional revenue.
- These other sources of revenue could be a carbon tax ($440 billion), a financial transaction tax ($350 billion), or taxing capital gains like ordinary income and creating new

upper tax brackets ($160 billion). Did you know that for fifty years—between 1932 and 1982—the top income tax rate averaged 82%? Our current highest rate is 39%.

- From 2008 to 2014, we created about $5 trillion out of thin air, and handed it to banks in hopes they would lend it to people. It was called quantitative easing. The result was rich people got even richer. Why not skip the banks, and just hand debt-free money directly and equally to all citizens? Potentially, a quarter of basic income could require no taxes at all.

- There is a place in the world that already pays a regular dividend to everyone living there, universally to child and adult, through a wealth fund it has created through royalty fees paid by companies for the rights to profit from its natural resources. This place is Alaska, and the "Alaska Model" could be applied anywhere as a means of granting a basic income as the social dividend from a sovereign wealth fund of resource-based revenue.

- We could even get more creative by thinking about how we go about giving away other forms of shared resources royalty-free to corporations, like the use of our public airwaves, and patents/copyrights that should have entered the public domain long ago but haven't thanks to corporate lobbying from those like Disney to protect their profits off of creations like Mickey Mouse. Did you know the Happy Birthday song isn't even in the public domain? Companies should pay us instead of politicians to keep things out of the public domain, and we could use this revenue as an additional means of growing a resource-based wealth fund.

Suffice to say, there exist plenty of funding options, any of which are more than sufficient, that if combined could potentially allow for a larger basic income, or a reduction or even elimination of income taxes entirely. And because we're already spending so much money on the costs of not having a basic income, we could actually even save more money than it costs.

Okay, It's Affordable... but Wouldn't People Stop Working?

We studied this question in the 1970s here in the United States, back when Guaranteed Annual Income (GAI) was a goal of President Nixon and the House even successfully passed a bill for it. The findings from the accompanying large-scale experiments done in cities like Seattle and Denver found that surprisingly, hardly anyone actually stopped working, and instead reduced their hours slightly, with men reducing their hours the least—by a maximum of 8%. This slight reduction in hours was then replicated to even less of a degree in Canada's Minimum Income (Mincome) experiment, with men choosing to work as little as 1% fewer hours.

Meanwhile, we find ourselves today working too much. Having drifted away from the 40-hour work week, we now find 1 out of every 3 of us working more than 50 hours, with many even working more than 60 hours. And what are the effects of this?

> New studies show that working more very seldom produces better results. Employees work many more hours now than they have in the past, but it's coming at the expense of health, happiness, and even productivity. While it looks good to be the first to arrive and the last to leave work each day, it turns out that putting in 60 hours of work each week may do more harm than good in achieving end results. Through the data, one thing becomes extremely clear: to boost productivity and foster excellent employees, the best thing businesses can do is to bring back the 40-hour work week.

We want to start working less. It would be good for overall productivity to be working less. In fact, in certain circumstances, we shouldn't even be working at all. It's called presenteeism, and happens when people refuse to call in sick.

> According to various studies, the total cost of presenteeism to U.S. employers falls anywhere between $150 billion to $250 billion each year, and those costs are on the rise as presenteeism becomes more frequent in tight economic times.

Right now people are going to work when they actually should not be going to work, and this is having a negative effect on the entire economy and even our overall health. We need people who are feeling sick to stay home when they should be staying home and not feeling forced to work because they absolutely have to earn that money, or out of fear of losing their jobs if they actually take a sick day.

It's kind of curious isn't it? Here we are worrying people will work less if we guarantee a basic income, and the reality of the situation is that people are presently working too much, and it is costing all of us. Combine this with the fact there's 2 people seeking every 1 available job, and the obvious solution is that we actually want people to be able to choose to work less, to free up more positions for those seeking jobs who are currently being excluded from the labor market.

But Still, What About Those Few Who WOULD Stop Working?

Through the elimination of the welfare trap thanks to basic income, this would mean that anyone choosing not to work—instead opting to just live off their basic incomes—would be earning less than everyone choosing to work for additional income. This could not only decrease unemployment and increase productivity, but simultaneously fix the situation we have right now, where it's possible for the unemployed to actually earn more in equivalent benefits than the cash incomes of those who are employed.

Plus, the very ability of people to not need a job, makes it that much harder for employers to exploit employees with insufficient wages and poor working conditions. The ability to actually say "No," means the empowerment of labor on an individual level—no unions required.

Simply Put, Basic Income Makes Work Actually Pay.

Wouldn't this simply just cause everything to cost more?

The question of basic income and rising prices is an equation with a lot of variables, but we should not forget that it would replace existing programs like food stamps and that competition would still exist. Raising prices in a world where everyone has more freedom of choice and purchasing power would likely result in people choosing more affordable competitors or becoming competitors themselves. Support for this was observed in a basic income experiment in India, where prices actually decreased.

> Another criticism is that a basic income would be inflationary. But it would be a substitute for more expensive policies. The criticism also neglects the elasticity of supply. Thus, it generated a sharp rise in food production, resulting in better nutrition and productivity and in lower unit prices.

Why Would (insert who you dislike) Ever Agree to This?

The idea of basic income cuts across all party lines. From the extreme right to the extreme left, we are hearing calls for basic income. Those on the right love its potential to shrink the size of government and do away with minimum wage laws, while those on the left love its potential to reduce inequality and once and for all put an end to poverty. Basic income is not "left" or "right." It's forward.

So Why Should You Support Unconditional Basic Income?

Why should you have supported the abolition of slavery back in the late 19th century? Why should you have supported the right for people other than rich white men to vote? Why should you have supported our landing on the Moon? Why should you have supported the ending of the Vietnam war, or the beginning of LBJ's war on poverty?

Because you want to make our world a better place. That's why.

> *"For several decades, our political system has promoted winner-loser inequality by emphasizing policies that favor corporate profits and high-income high wealth households at the expense of the middle class."*

Reducing the Wealth Gap Will Benefit Our Institutions

Gerald D. Jaynes

In the following viewpoint, Gerald D. Jaynes argues that rising inequality has concentrated too much political power at the top levels of government. Economic policies of the last few decades have emphasized policies that favor high-income and high-wealth households at the expense of the middle class. Jaynes recommends increases to the minimum wage and reforms to the income tax structures as a way of reversing income inequality. Jaynes is a professor of economics and African American studies at Yale University.

"Rising Inequality and Middle Class Stagnation: A Growing Threat to American Democracy and Economic Prosperity," Gerald D. Jaynes, Prof. Economics, Yale University, February 24, 2015. Reprinted by permission.

As you read, consider the following questions:

1. According to Jaynes, how have American economic policies put downward pressures on the demand for labor?
2. According to Jaynes, what has been the impact of tax cuts to high-income households and corporations?
3. What policies does the author propose to benefit low- and middle-income households?

Thank you Senator Warren and Congressman Cummings for bringing us together to discuss this most important topic.

I begin with an observation. The nation's growing concern with inequality is not against inequality per se. Americans accept inequality as a necessary platform to provide economic opportunity and incentives for efficient allocation of talents and skills. Americans generally favor structuring institutions so the opportunity to amass large wealth flourishes. The fact that incomes are rising at unprecedented rates among the upper reaches of the income distribution would not evoke concern among most Americans if the standards of living among the middle-class and below were also improving. However, living standards for the middle class are stagnating and for some Americans even deteriorating.

Contemporary inequality has the distasteful odor of a winner-loser economy. An economy governed by a political-economic system that, for several decades now, rewards income elites who gain at everyone else's expense. With the exception of the late 1990s, middle class versions of the American Dream have been deferred instead of flourishing. Winner-loser inequality harbors deadly implications for the health of our economy and democratic institutions. Rising incomes at the top accompanied by stagnation and deterioration for middle and lower income households concentrates too much political power at the top. It also undermines the middle class purchasing power on which our prosperity rests.

Globalization's Pressure on the Supply and Demand for Labor

The winner-loser inequality threatening our society is indicative of a dramatic shift in the manner by which market and political institutions are allocating rewards. The shift is due to a combination of economic forces *and* political *choices*! During the last several decades, nearly all economic and political forces have put downward pressure on the demand for labor at middle and low quintiles of the wage distribution. Gathered under the convenient umbrella term globalization, the factors behind the lagging demand for such labor are well known even if their relative importance is not. Computer driven technological change replacing labor with machines, cheap imports produced by low-wage foreign workers, and out-sourcing have each reduced the demand for domestic workers. Contemporaneous with downward pressure on the demand for labor, other factors have put outward pressure on labor supply. Perhaps the most important factor expanding the supply of labor at lower wages than would otherwise have occurred is the decline of unions due to the weakened demand for domestic labor *and* vigorous anti-union activities of both corporate America and government.

However, winner-loser inequality is not simply the effects of global market trends over which the nation has little control. For several decades, our political system has promoted winner-loser inequality by emphasizing policies that favor corporate profits and high-income high wealth households at the expense of the middle class. Perhaps the two most obvious indicators of government's complicity in winner-loser inequality are its policies toward the minimum wage and income taxes. A minimum wage whose purchasing power has deteriorated to pre-1980 levels combined with four huge tax cuts since 1980 favoring high income, and especially capital gains, accompanied by runaway deregulation of industry easily differentiate the emphasis behind government policy before and after the late 1970s.

Proponents of these policies have promised growth and prosperity with each tax cut and deregulation. However, experience shows, trickle-down to the middle-class promises of tax-cuts for the rich merely enrich the rich. Rather than increasing investment in capital and infrastructure that increases labor productivity and wages, deregulated financial institutions and markets, combined with low capital gains taxes have driven up returns to nonproductive assets distorting incentives in financial markets and creating debacles such as the recent housing bubble and Great Recession. Unprecedented current profits hide substantial long-term social costs.

Facts of Winner-Loser Inequality

A few simple facts are sufficient to substantiate the dangerous trend of inequality and the failure of the tax-cut low-wage policies. Observing trends over approximately the last three and a half decades from 1980 to 2013, in 2013-inflation-constant-dollars:

- The share of household income received by the middle 60% of households fell from 51.7% to 45.8%, while the share to the top 20% increased from 44.1% to 51%.

You heard me right, the top 20% of households receives more than half of all household income. Moreover, gains of higher income households at the expense of the middle class were even more pronounced at the highest and lowest income levels.

- The share received by the top 5% of households rose from 16.5% to 22.2%.
- The Share received by the bottom 20% fell from 4.2% to 3.2%.

The pronounced redistribution of income from the bottom and middle sectors of the distribution to households at the top can only occur if incomes are growing much faster at the top.

- The mean income of the 20% of households exactly in the *middle* of the distribution grew less than one-third of one-percent per annum from $47,645 to $52,322.

- The mean income of the top 5% grew almost 7 times more per annum virtually exploding from $187,023 to $322,343.

For middle class households, income is almost completely composed of wages. Because the wages of men at the middle of the wage distribution actually deteriorated, middle class households were able to see even these very small gains only because of the well-known increase in labor force participation of women (especially married women).

- Between 1979 and 2014, median wages of full-time year round-workers have stagnated.

Weekly wages of men declined from a 1979 peak of $952 to $871 in 2014; women's weekly 5 wages increased from $593 to $719, but have changed little during the past decade. During 2014 both men's and women's median wages show modest increases. These developments bode very badly for middle class retirement prospects

- The top 20% of households in the income distribution hold about 72% of total savings in retirement accounts.
- Most Americans approaching retirement have little or nothing saved in retirement accounts. In 2010, 40 percent of families in their peak saving years (age 55–64) had nothing saved in retirement accounts and 10 percent had $12,000 or less according to data from the Federal Reserve Survey of Consumer Finances.

Why Is Winner-Loser Inequality Bad for the Economy

The middle class forms the numerical and cultural backbone of our economic and political institutions. As the slow recovery from the Great Recession demonstrates, a middle class with stagnant incomes puts severe downward pressure on macroeconomic demand for goods and services. Consumption demand underpinned by millions of middle class households with adequate disposable income is an essential key to our prosperity. The economy cannot thrive without this demand. The top 5 or 10 percent income households are too small in number to replace healthy middle class demand. Furthermore, increased exports could provide the needed demand only if inequality in our wage structure increases even more dramatically creating a nation of haves and have-nots that will threaten our democratic institutions in ways to horrible to contemplate.

Policy Recommendations

Minimum wage—Our first policy priority should be to increase the minimum wage. An increase in the minimum wage will have immediate effects on the well-being of many lower income households. Moreover, through its upward pressure on employers' relative wage structure, an increase in the minimum wage will benefit middle class households above minimum wage levels.

Tight Labor Market—We must also pursue tight labor markets with unemployment below 5%.

Tax reform—It is time for a serious discussion about subsuming unemployment and social security taxes within the general income tax both for persons and corporations. Removing these taxes from employers' wage bill should have a positive effect on both employment and wages. Moreover, if the transfer into the general income tax is done in a manner introducing greater progressivity into the overall tax system, the change will also increase middle class paychecks. This transfer can be accomplished with minimal change in existing administration of social security and unemployment systems by maintaining the same accounting system as is now used with individuals' paychecks. Both employees and employers will have paper accounts as they do now, but the funds paying for the programs will be earmarked funds from the income tax.

Periodical and Internet Sources Bibliography

The following articles have been selected to supplement the diverse views presented in this chapter.

Anna Barford and Kate Pickett, "How to Build a More Equal American Society: Lessons from Successful Experiences," *Solutions*, July 2014.

Dietrick Domanski, Michela Scatigna, and Anna Zabai, "Wealth Inequality and Monetary Policy," BIS *Quarterly Review*, March 2016.

Josh Kraushaar, "The Proven Way to Fight Income Inequality: Education," *The Atlantic*, January 7, 2014.

Robert Kuttner, "Education Alone Is Not the Answer to Income Inequality and Slow Recovery," *The American Prospect*, August 14, 2014.

Dylan Matthew, "Ten Ways to Reduce Inequality Without Raising Tax Rates," *The Washington Post*, December 6, 2012.

Clifton B. Parker, "Tax Reform Could Reduce Wealth Inequality Gap, Stanford Scholar Says," *Stanford News*, January 27, 2015.

Kate Pickett, "5 Reasons Why We Need to Reduce Global Inequality," World Economic Forum, September 22, 2015.

Robert B. Reich, "How to Shrink Inequality," *Nation*, May 26, 2014.

Sheldon Richman, "Two Kinds of Income Inequality," Future of Freedom Foundation, January 22, 2015.

Jeanne Sahadi, "Will a Higher Minimum Wage Really Reduce Income Inequality? *CNN Money*, January 15, 2014.

Noah Smith, "How to Fix America's Wealth Inequality: Teach Americans to Be Cheap," *The Atlantic*, March 12, 2013.

CHAPTER 4

Does America's Wealth Gap Harm Society?

Chapter Preface

The 2010 release of a report by the US Congress Joint Economic Committee announced some alarming news for people concerned about income inequality. Titled *Income Inequality and the Great Recession*, the report contained data showing the relationship between income inequality and economic crises. According to the report, "Peaks in income inequality preceded both the Great Depression and the Great Recession, suggesting that high levels of income inequality may destabilize the economy as a whole." In fact, the report concluded, income inequality might have been the root cause of the Great Depression of the 1930s and 2007–2009 recession.

The income inequality report takes a historical view of income inequality. In 1928, at the height of the Roaring Twenties stock market bubble, the share of income in the US going to the top 10 percent of wage earners peaked at 49.3 percent. Eighty years later, in the year before the 2007–2009 recession, the share of income held by the wealthiest 10 percent again peaked at over 49 percent. During the Great Recession, depressed average household incomes pushed more people into poverty. The report points out that during the thirty years preceding the Great Recession, incomes for the top 20 percent of Americans grew 70 percent larger. In contrast, income growth for middle wage earners was only 25.7 percent.

Some economists think that severe income inequality makes the economy more vulnerable to recessions. Before the Great Recession, stagnant middle-class incomes increased demand for credit. With access to easy borrowing, consumers racked up debt to pay for housing, consumer goods, and college educations. Wealthy households, on the other hand, were able to invest more into financial markets, some of which were unregulated and high risk. The economy collapsed when consumers could not keep pace with their debt and the financial markets, based on a speculative housing bubble, could not absorb their losses.

One of the biggest casualties of income inequality, said President Barack Obama in a 2013 speech, is loss of upward mobility. He talked about the American Dream "where even if you're born with nothing, with a little hard work you can improve your own situation over time and build something better to leave your kids." However, he said, that dream may have ended. He quoted statistics showing that children born in the top 20 percent had a 2-in-3 chance of staying there. On the other hand, children born into poverty had less than a 1-in-20 chance at entering the top income levels.

The articles that follow reflect a range of viewpoints about the impact of income and wealth inequality. Some experts argue that rising inequality leads to higher standards of living for the rest of the society. Others point to globalization, the movement of factory jobs to third world countries, and the decline of labor unions as having a greater impact on the economy than the wealth gap. Some economists link an increase in crime and a decline in health to income inequality. As the authors of these articles demonstrate, there are a variety of answers to the question of whether income inequality harms society.

> *"What unites areas of low mobility ...*
> *are broken family structures, reduced*
> *levels of civic and community*
> *engagement, lower-quality*
> *K-12 education, greater racial and*
> *economic segregation, and broader*
> *income inequality."*

Income Inequality Is Difficult to Reverse

Christina Pazzanese

In the following viewpoint, Christina Pazzanese claims that the most damaging aspect of the current income inequality in the US is that the 1 percent holds increasing political and economic power over the rest of society. She contends that the wealthy class has the greatest access to the educational resources that can improve upward mobility. She suggests that the best place to begin reducing inequality is at the state and local levels. Pazzanese is a staff writer for the Harvard Gazette.

"The Rich and the Rest," by Christina Pazzanese, From Harvard Gazette, February 9, 2016.

As you read, consider the following questions:

1. What examples does the author use to illustrate the areas where middle and lower classes feel the impact of inequality in their daily lives?
2. According to Pazzanese, how has the Supreme Court decision on campaign finance laws impacted the amount of power controlled by the 1 percent?
3. What are some of the characteristics that unite areas in the country with low economic mobility, according to the author?

W e can either have democracy in this country or we can have great wealth concentrated in the hands of a few, but we can't have both," Associate Supreme Court Justice Louis Brandeis said decades ago during another period of pronounced inequality in America.

Echoing the concern of the Harvard Law School graduate, over the last 30 years myriad forces have battered the United States' legendary reputation as the world's "land of opportunity."

The 2008 global economic meltdown that bailed out Wall Street financiers but left ordinary citizens to fend for themselves trained a spotlight on the unfairness of fiscal inequality. The issue gained traction during the Occupy Wall Street protest movement in 2011 and during the successful U.S. Senate campaign of former Harvard Law School Professor Elizabeth Warren in 2012.

What was once viewed as a fringe political issue is now at the heart of the angry, populist rhetoric of the 2016 presidential campaign. Personified by outsider candidates Bernie Sanders and Donald Trump, economic inequality has resonated with broad swaths of nervous voters on both the left and right.

Lawrence Katz, the Elisabeth Allison Professor of Economics in Harvard's Faculty of Arts and Sciences, says the most damaging aspects of the gap between the top 1 percent of Americans and everyone else involve the increasing economic and political power that the very rich wield over society, along with a growing educational divide and escalating social segregation in which the elites live in literal and figurative gated communities.

If the rate of economic mobility—the ability of people to improve their economic station—was higher, he says, our growing income disparity might not be such a problem.

"But what we have been seeing is rising inequality with stagnant mobility, which means that the consequences of where you start out, whether it's in a poor neighborhood, whether it's from a single-parent household, are more consequential today than in the past. Your ZIP code and the exact characteristics of your parents seem to matter more," said Katz. "And that's quite disturbing."

The growing gap between the rich and the rest isn't a matter of who can afford a yacht or a Manhattan penthouse, analysts say. Rather, it's the crippling nature of these disparities as they touch nearly every aspect of daily lives, from career prospects and educational opportunities to health risks and neighborhood safety.

The widening income gap also has fueled a class-based social disconnect that has produced inequitable educational results. "Now, your family income matters more than your own abilities in terms of whether you complete college," said Robert Putnam, the Peter and Isabel Malkin Professor of Public Policy at Harvard Kennedy School. "Smart poor kids are less likely to graduate from college now than dumb rich kids. That's not because of the schools, that's because of all the advantages that are available to rich kids."

Economic inequality also feeds the political, driving everything from the actions of our political representatives to the quality and quantity of civic engagement, such as voting and community-based public service.

"It's long been known that the better educated, those with higher incomes, participate more" in politics on "everything from voting to contacting politicians to donating," said Theda Skocpol, the Victor S. Thomas Professor of Government and Sociology at Harvard's Faculty of Arts and Sciences. "What is quite new in recent times is … very systematically, that government really responds much more to the privileged than to even middle-income people who vote."

Money Eases Access

The U.S. Supreme Court's unlacing of campaign-finance laws that limited how much donors could give candidates or affiliate organizations, coupled with allowing donors to shield their identities from public scrutiny, have spawned a financial arms race that requires viable presidential candidates, for example, to solicit donors constantly in a quest to raise $1 billion or more to win.

Given that rulebook, it's hardly surprising that the political supporters with the greatest access to candidates are usually the very wealthy. Backers with both influence and access often help to shape the political agenda. The result is a kind of velvet rope that can keep those without economic clout on the sidelines, out of the conversation.

"Something like the carried-interest provision in the tax code, when you explain it to ordinary citizens, they don't like the idea that income earned by investing other people's money should be taxed at a lower rate than regular wage and salary income. It's not popular in some broad, polling sense. But many politicians probably don't realize it at all because ... politicians spend a lot of their time asking people to give money to them [who] don't think it's a good idea to change that," said Skocpol. "There's a real danger that, as wealth and income are more and more concentrated toward the top, that it does become a vicious circle."

"Money has corrupted our political process," said Lawrence Lessig, the Roy L. Furman Professor of Law and Leadership at Harvard Law School. In Congress, he said, "They focus too much on the tiny slice, 1 percent, who are funding elections. In the current election cycle [as of October], 158 families have given half the money to candidates. That's a banana republic democracy; that's not an American democracy."

Lessig was so unhappy with how political campaigns are funded that he briefly ran for president on the issue. Reviewing his efforts during a Harvard forum on the topic in November, he described his candidacy as a referendum on the campaign-finance system, but also on the need to reform Congress, which he called a "broken and corrupted institution" undercut by big donors and gerrymandered election districts.

How We Got Here

Christopher "Sandy" Jencks, the Malcolm Wiener Professor of Social Policy at Harvard Kennedy School, believes that the last 30 years of rising American inequality can be attributed to three key factors:

- The decline in jobs and employment rates for less-skilled workers, which has increased the number of households with children but no male breadwinner.
- The demand for college graduates outpacing the pool of job candidates, adding to the gap between the middle class and upper-middle class.
- The share of income gains flowing to the top 1 percent of earners doubling as a result of deregulation, globalization, and speculation in the financial-services industry.

The U.S. government does "considerably less" than comparable democracies to even out disposable family incomes, Jencks says. And current state and local tax policies "actually increase income inequality."

"All the costs and risks of capitalism seem to have been shifted largely to those who work rather than those who invest," he said.

Compounding the economic imbalance is the unlikely prospect that those at the bottom can ever improve their lot.

"We have some of the lowest rates of upward mobility of any developed country in the world," said Nathaniel Hendren, an associate professor of economics at Harvard's Faculty of Arts and Sciences who has studied intergenerational mobility and how inequality transmits across generations.

Hendren, along with Harvard economists Katz and Raj Chetty, now at Stanford University, looked at the lasting effects of moving children to better neighborhoods as part of Moving to Opportunity, a short-lived federal housing program from the '90s. Their analysis, published in May, found that the longer children are exposed to better environments, the better they do economically in the future. Whichever city or state children grow up in also radically affects whether they'll move out of poverty, he said.

For children in parts of the Midwest, the Northeast and the West, upward mobility rates are high. But in the South and portions of the Rust Belt, rates are very low. For example, a child born in Iowa into a household making less than $25,000 a year has an 18 percent chance to move into the upper 20 percent of income strata over a lifetime. But a child born in Atlanta or Charlotte, North Carolina, has only a 4 percent chance of moving up, their study found.

What unites areas of low mobility, Hendren says, are broken family structures, reduced levels of civic and community engagement, lower-quality K-12 education, greater racial and economic segregation, and broader income inequality.

In addition, 90 percent of American workers have seen their wages stall while their costs of living continue to rise.

"When you look at the data, it's sobering. Median household income when last reported in 2013 was at a level first attained in 1989, adjusting for inflation. That's a long time to go without any gains," said Jan Rivkin, the Bruce V. Rauner Professor of Business Administration at Harvard Business School.

Wage inequality is on the rise for both genders. Within that range, the gap between men and women remains a hot-button issue despite gains by women in the last three decades. Broadly, the ratio of median earnings for women increased from 0.56 to 0.78 between 1970 and 2010.

But according to Claudia Goldin, the Henry Lee Professor of Economics at Harvard's Faculty of Arts & Sciences, the gender earnings gap is not a constant, varying widely by occupation and age. While women in their late 20s earn about 92 percent of what their male counterparts earn, women in their early 50s earn just 71 cents on the dollar that the average man makes. For some career paths, like pharmacists, veterinarians and optometrists, corporatization has closed the gap between men and women. Even so, wiping away the gender pay gap isn't a cure-all for inequality.

"If you reduce gender inequality to zero, you've closed inequality … by a very small percent," said Goldin. "I'm not saying there aren't things that we can't fix, but I am telling you, without a doubt, they're going to move the lever by very little."

Underinvestment in "The Commons"

Rivkin says that the pressures of globalization and technological change and the weakening of labor unions have had a major impact. But he disagrees that political favoritism toward business interests and away from ordinary citizens is the primary reason for burgeoning inequality. Rather, he says that sustained underinvestment by government and business in "the commons"— the institutions and services that offer wide community benefits, like schools and roads—has been especially detrimental.

Last spring, Harvard Business School conducted an alumni survey for its annual U.S. Competitiveness Project research series, probing respondents for their views on the current and future state of American businesses, their prospects of dominating the global marketplace, and the likelihood that the resulting prosperity would be shared more evenly among citizens.

The survey findings, released in September, showed that most HBS alumni were skeptical that living standards would rise more equitably soon, given existing policies and practices. A majority said that inequality and related issues like rising poverty, limited economic mobility, and middle-class stagnation were not only social ills, but problems that affected their businesses.

"My sense is that a larger and larger number of business leaders are waking up to the idea that issues of inequality, and particularly lack of shared prosperity, have to be addressed for the sake of business," said Rivkin, the project's co-chair.

The surging power of the wealthy in America now rivals levels last seen in the Gilded Age of the late 19th century, analysts say. One difference, however, is that the grotesque chasm between that era's robber barons and tenement dwellers led to major social and policy reforms that are still with us, including labor rights, women's suffrage and federal regulatory agencies to oversee trade, banking, food and drugs.

Hendren said there's no less chance today of rising or falling along the income spectrum than there was 25 years ago. "The chances of moving up or down the ladder are the same," he said, "but the way we think about inequality is that the rungs on the ladder have gotten wider. The difference between being at the top versus the bottom of the income distribution is wider, so the consequences of being born to a poor family in dollar terms are wider."

What Price Inaction?

Unless America's policymakers begin to chip away at the underlying elements of inequality, the costs to the nation will be profound, analysts say.

"I think we will pay many prices. We will continue to have divisive politics. We won't make the investments we need to provide the majority of kids with a better life, and that would be really not fulfilling," said Katz.

Partisan gridlock in Washington, D.C., has diminished the effectiveness of government—perhaps the most essential and powerful tool for addressing inequality and addressing citizens' needs. By adopting a political narrative that government should not and cannot effectively solve problems, legislative inaction results in policy inaction.

"It's definitely been a strategy" to justify starving government of resources, which in turn weakens it and makes it less attractive as a tool to accomplish big things, said Skocpol. "In an everybody-for-themselves situation, it is the better-educated and the wealthy who can protect themselves."

Surveying the landscape, Katz sees reasons to be both hopeful and worried.

"The optimism is that there are regions of the U.S., metropolitan areas that have tremendous upward mobility. So we do have models that work. We do have programs like Medicare and the Earned Income Tax Credit that work pretty well. I think that if national policy more approximated the upper third of state and local policies, the U.S. would have a lot of hope," said Katz. "My pessimistic take would be that if you look at two thirds of America, things are not improving in the way we would like."

Putnam is heartened that inequality has been widely recognized as a major problem and is no longer treated as a fringe political issue.

What Can Be Done?

Jencks says there are many steps the federal government could take—if there was the political will to do so—to slow down or reverse inequality, like increasing the minimum wage, revising the tax code to tax corporate profits and investments more, reducing the debt burden on college students and improving K-12 education so more students are prepared for college and for personal advancement.

"Strong regulation and strong support for collective control over the things that society values is much more prevalent in societies that have lower levels of inequality," he said.

Though labor rights have been eroding for decades, Benjamin Sachs, the Kestnbaum Professor of Labor and Industry at Harvard Law School, still thinks that unions could provide an unusual way to help equalize political power nationally. For decades, unions wielded both economic and political clout, but legislative and court decisions reduced their effectiveness as economic actors, cutting their political influence as well. At the same time, campaign finance reform efforts to limit the influence of wealth on politics have failed.

To restore some balance, Sachs suggests "unbundling" unions' political and economic activities, allowing them to serve as political organizing vehicles for low- and middle-income Americans, even those whom a union may not represent for collective bargaining purposes.

"The risk that economic inequalities will produce political ones ... has led to several generations of campaign finance regulation designed to get money out of politics. But these efforts have not succeeded," Sachs wrote in a 2013 Yale Law Review article. "Rather than struggling to find new ways to restrict political spending by the wealthy ... the unbundled union, in which political organization is liberated from collective bargaining, constitutes one promising component of such a broader attempt to improve representational equality."

Still, given the present trend lines, Goldin said the economic forces that perpetuate unequal wages—and inequality more broadly—won't simply disappear even with a spate of new laws.

"I think it is naïve of most individuals to think that for everything there is something that government can legislate and regulate and impose that makes life better for everybody," she said. "That's just not the case."

Even so, with Congress stalled over fresh policies, analysts say that much of the innovation concerning inequality has moved to state and local levels, where partisanship is less calcified and the needs of constituents are more evident.

In Oregon and California, for example, residents will be automatically registered to vote upon turning 18, a move that Skocpol says should bolster civic participation and provide protection from onerous new voter-identification laws.

While it's clear that investing in children and their education pays lifelong dividends for them, those gains take 20 years to be realized, said Katz. That's why it's critical that their parents get help and live in less vulnerable situations.

"There is certainly evidence that if we reduce the degree of economic and racial and ethnic segregation of our communities, we can move in that direction," said Katz, who is working on an experiment to expand the Earned Income Tax Credit in New York City to help younger workers without children who are struggling to break into the labor market.

Changes to the minimum wage, the tax system, and the treatment of carried interest "are all debates in which our society should engage," said Rivkin, who cautioned that those would be hard-fought political battles that wouldn't yield results for at least a decade.

Of course industry needs to run its businesses productively and profitably, but it can do so without harming "the commons," Rivkin said. "Business has been very effective at pursuing its narrow self-interest in looking for special tax breaks. I think that kind of behavior just needs to stop." Drawing on an idea from Harvard Business School finance Professor Mihir Desai, Rivkin suggests that businesses treat their tax responsibilities as a compliance function rather than as a profit center. That money could then go back into investment in "the commons," where "lots of common ground" exists among business, labor, policymakers, educators and others.

"The businesses should be working with the local community college to train the workers whom they would love to hire; the university should be getting together with policymakers to figure out how to get innovations out of the research lab into startups faster; business should work with educators to reinvent the school system," said Rivkin.

Putnam suggests more widespread mentoring of low-income children who lack the social safety net that upper- and middle-class children enjoy, a topic he explored in "Our Kids."

He recently convened five working groups to develop a series of white papers that will offer overviews of the key challenges in family structure and parenting; early childhood development; K-12 education; vocational, technical and community colleges; and community institutions. The papers will be shared with mayors and leaders in churches, nonprofits, and community organizations across the nation, where much of the reform effort is taking place.

"There's an increasing sense that this is a big deal, that we're moving toward an America that none of us has ever lived in, a world of two Americas, a completely economically divided country," said Putnam. "That's not an America I want my grandchildren to grow up in. And I think there are lots of people in America who, if they stop and think about it, would say, 'No, that's not really us.'"

> "Greater income inequality can
> amplify political tensions by
> raising polarization."

A Wealth Gap Creates Political Division

Christos Makridis

In the following viewpoint, Christos Makridis argues that income disparity in the United States creates political polarization, which, in turn, affects the progress of the nation. Political polarization can lead to government gridlock, making it all but impossible for lawmakers to work together to pass legislation. Makridis is a Ph.D. Candidate in Labor and Public Economics at Stanford University.

As you read, consider the following questions:

1. What is the author's central argument?
2. Can the author prove causality in his argument about income inequality's effect on political polarization?
3. What are the dangers of political polarization?

Political polarization today is greater than it's been in recent history – at least since the 1970s. To see that, one need only look at the current U.S. presidential election.

And whatever your political leanings, an overly divided country can hamper its progress, such as the ability to innovate or adapt to geopolitical risk.

Another trend that has emerged over the same period is the widening gap between the richest and poorest Americans. By some estimates, it's the widest it's ever been.

These two coinciding facts raise the tantalizing question: Did the rise of income inequality over the past three decades contribute to increased political polarization? Or is it the other way around? Or perhaps it's just a coincidence that they both have climbed over the same 30-40 year period?

Chicken and the Egg?

Unfortunately, causality – and its direction – can be very difficult to show, although intuitively we can see how either one might affect the other.

For example, greater income inequality may generate more polarization because disparities in earnings affect our priorities. It's been argued that as we make more or less money, the issues we care about most change, as do how we feel about those issues.

On the other hand, greater polarization can generate gridlock in government, making it more difficult to pass legislation. If, for example, there are pressing issues, then greater dispersion in attitudes might make agreement more difficult. Inaction could, in theory, curtail efforts aimed at addressing inequality.

While both are plausible, my view is that the former mechanism is more likely – greater income inequality is leading to more polarization – because earnings inequality is not a transitory relationship. Rather, big differences in earnings takes years to develop, and the bulk of income inequality is explained by longer-run factors. For causality to work the other way, contemporary polarized voting patterns would have to be affecting inequality, which seems unlikely.

Furthermore, recent research in political science has also pushed back on conventional theories that polarization hinders the passage of policy.

Understanding the direction of causality is important for policy. If income inequality is the cause, we should not expect political compromises until labor force participation and competitiveness rise – reducing inequality. If polarization is the cause, then we should not expect our economy to improve until we are able to compromise.

Diving into the Data

These questions prompted me to gather data from the Current Population Survey (CPS) and Gallup from 2008 to 2015.

The CPS is a survey frequently used by economists to understand changing demographics and employment outcomes throughout the U.S. economy with fresh snapshots every month. The Bureau of Labor Statistics uses the data to compile its monthly unemployment report.

Gallup, arguably the largest polling organization in the U.S., regularly surveys individuals on a range of issues, including their political ideology.

Before we go any further, we need to agree on some definitions. First, although political polarization does not have a uniform definition, I define it here as the fraction of people reporting that they are extreme liberal minus those reporting as extreme conservative, state by state. By taking the difference between the two opposite sides of the spectrum, the measure captures the dispersion that exist at a state level. In other words, the measure is not merely meant to pick up whether a state is Republican or Democrat, but rather the dispersion of attitudes.

Second, income inequality in economics is typically measured by the labor earnings gap between those at the top and bottom 10 percent (90-10 gap) or between the top 10 percent and the bottom 50 percent (90-50 gap). I'll be using a version of that, which employs natural logarithms, here.

What the Data Show

Combining all these data, I found that states showing greater degrees of political polarization are associated with higher levels of income inequality.

In particular, a 1 percent rise in the 90-10 earnings gap is associated with a 0.18 percentage point increase in political polarization – that is, the share of individuals identifying as extreme liberals minus those reporting as extreme conservatives goes up by that amount. For the 90-50 earnings gap, it's 0.22 percentage point.

The states that have the greatest income inequality, like Washington, D.C., are also the states with the greatest polarization, according to these data. In fact, the 90-10 earnings gap over this 2008-2015 period explains approximately 27 percent of what we're seeing in political polarization.

In other words, the evidence indicates not only a strong correlation between income inequality and political polarization but also potential causality: Greater income inequality can amplify political tensions by raising polarization. These results imply that income inequality can indirectly affect economic outcomes by increasing the fraction of people who identify as extreme liberal.

What could explain the economically and statistically significant relationship between income inequality and political polarization? To delve further into the possible mechanisms, I also extracted individual-level data from the American Time Use Survey, together with state-level data on unemployment rates.

The goal here is to understand how different dimensions of labor market outcomes – besides income inequality – might be related to polarization. One possibility, for example, is that the experience of underemployment generates apathy about the political and economic system. These experiences could affects individuals' views about what parties should do for them.

There are two different relationships to highlight: higher levels of polarization are associated with lower average hours worked per week as well as higher unemployment. In particular, a one percentage point rise in our polarization metric is associated with 15 hours less of work per week, on average, and 6 percent greater unemployment.

The fact that areas with greater unemployment or underemployment also tend to be more polarized and, in particular, likely to lean extreme left suggests that an individual's experience in the labor market could exert a strong influence on her political ideology. In other words, poor labor market outcomes might inflict more harm on a geography than just the direct impact on individual's economic situation. They may also create a more polarized social and political environment.

With these results in mind, there are three caveats to consider. First, they are not necessarily causal. There are still statistical concerns about why we observe polarization and inequality changing in the data.

Second, while the data used here span from 2008 to 2015, the past decade may feature a very different relationship between inequality and polarization.

Third, although my measure of political polarization is reasonable and robust to an alternative definition that simply separates between extreme Democrats and extreme Republicans, it is also possible that the relationships here may be weaker or switched under alternative definitions of polarization.

Unintended Consequences

We all realize that greater inequality has tangible implications for who wins and loses in society. However, all these pieces of evidence suggest it may also induce more extreme political attitudes and ideologies.

For example, the popularity of "free college" among Bernie Sanders supporters –and the fact that it affected Hillary Clinton's platform – reflects precisely this phenomenon, despite the fact that there was not any serious economic rationale behind it.

Political polarization can have a number of adverse consequences, ranging from difficulty in passing legislation to unpredictability in domestic and foreign policy.

Predictability is important for a number of reasons. For example, in monetary policy, having a predictable rule that governs how the Federal Reserve adjusts interest rates has been shown to positively affect economic activity (known as the Taylor Rule). Policy uncertainty can also help explain the economy's booms and busts. And, finally, predictability and continuity in policy also affect the United States' credibility abroad.

If my descriptive evidence here is right, it underscores the importance of serious policies aimed at tackling inequality in ways that raise everyone's opportunity. That means focusing on how we can make the pie bigger, rather than how to better split it up.

And, by addressing income inequality, we might also indirectly help mend some of the political fractures that have emerged in recent years.

> *"If we're serious about reducing
> inequality, we need to help people
> earn the kind of living that enables
> them to provide for their families and
> build a better future."*

The Wealth Gap Diminishes Opportunity

Lawrence Mishel

In the following viewpoint, Lawrence Mishel argues that intergenerational mobility is strongly linked to income inequality. He contends that high executive pay and an advantageous financial sector is responsible for the high-income growth of the 1 percent. He proposes the improvement of educational opportunities for the lower classes as a way to increase opportunities for upward mobility. Mishel is president of the Economic Policy Institute.

"If we want to improve upward mobility, we must tackle income inequality," by Lawrence Mishel, President, Economic Policy Institute, March 17, 2016. https://www.fordfoundation.org/ideas/equals-change-blog/posts/if-we-want-to-improve-upward-mobility-we-must-tackle-income-inequality. Licensed under CC BY 4.0.

As you read, consider the following questions:

1. According to the author, what reasons do conservatives give for the lower classes' lack of upward mobility?
2. What comprises the author's "opportunity agenda" to increase upward mobility?
3. According to the author, why is reducing income inequality essential for improving upward mobility?

Is America still the land of opportunity? Today in particular, it's a question well worth asking. The United States has low rates of upward mobility compared to other advanced nations, and there has been no improvement in decades. So creating more opportunity—and perhaps a better chance at that mobility—is a worthy goal.

But, opportunity simply doesn't thrive amid great inequalities. And so if "more opportunity" is offered as an alternative to addressing income inequality, it's a dodge. It's a hollow promise.

To understand why, it's important to appreciate the difference between opportunity—that is, upward mobility—and income inequality. Concerns about mobility center on strengthening the chances that children who grow up with relatively low incomes will attain middle-class or higher incomes in adulthood. Taking on inequality means focusing on whether low- and middle-income households improve their share of the economic growth generated in the next two decades. These are different issues—although ultimately they are intimately related.

To grasp the reality of rising inequality, take a look at what's happened to the share of the growth of household income received by the top 1 percent of our society. In 1979, this stratum received 9 percent of all income. Yet, between that year and 2007, the share of new income going to the 1 percent was 38 percent, according to the Congressional Budget Office—and estimates using tax data on new market-based incomes put it at 60 percent. In short, the

AMERICANS UNCONCERNED ABOUT INCOME INEQUALITY

President Obama put income inequality back in the news with a speech Wednesday saying the nation must address the growing gap between rich and poor. In most advanced countries, there is a correlation between public concern about the rich-poor gap and the underlying economic reality. But in the U.S., compared to the other wealthy nations surveyed, the disconnect between public concern and the size of the gap is large... Americans in the upper fifth of the income stream make 16.7 times the income of those in the lower fifth. Yet barely half (47%) of Americans think that the rich-poor gap is a very big problem for the U.S.

Separate Pew Research surveys in the U.S. alone have shown that whether or not Americans consider income inequality a big problem, they are indeed aware of the issue. About two-thirds (65%) said in a July 2012 poll that the gap between rich and poor had become larger over the preceding 10 years, and 57% of those who gave that answer thought that this was a bad thing for society. A survey conducted in April of that year found that 76% of Americans agreed with the statement that "today it's really true that the rich just get richer while the poor get poorer."

"The U.S.'s High Income Gap Is Met with Relatively Low Public Concern," by Bruce Stokes, December 6, 2013.

top 1 percent received four to six times its expected share of all the income growth.

For politicians who don't want to tackle income inequality, the opportunity dodge is very popular. Most conservatives consider income outcomes to be the result of meritocracy. "I don't care about income inequality per se; I care about opportunity inequality," Arthur Brooks, head of the American Enterprise Institute said last year. "I want everybody to have a chance to be mobile, to rise, for everybody to have a chance to earn success." Though left unsaid, this view rests on a perception that groups on the short end of income inequality haven't exerted sufficient effort, have inadequate skills, or have made counterproductive choices, such as not getting married. In other words, this perspective relies on blaming the victim.

Centrists also sometimes address opportunity instead of income inequality to avoid confronting the top 1 percent's capture of the lion's share of income growth. Addressing soaring executive pay and a runaway financial sector—the main causes of the 1 percent's income gains—is uncomfortable for centrists, as it necessarily involves redistribution; and besides, those folks are their donor base. And talking about opportunity allows a politician to avoid confronting ongoing wage suppression and the imbalance of bargaining power that has led to stagnant wages for college and non-college graduates alike over the last dozen years. As Rep. Scott Peters of the House New Democrat Coalition said last year, "To the extent that Republicans beat up on workers and Democrats beat up on employers—I'm not sure that offers voters much of a vision."

So let's be clear: The "opportunity agenda" of improved early-childhood education and access to college *will* help today's children to prosper as adults if coupled with policies that improve the availability of good jobs. But it will do nothing to enable today's families to share more fully in economic growth. That's what makes it a dodge to pursue opportunity while ignoring income inequality. At best, it's changing the subject—in Larry Summers's characterization, evading the tougher issue of who has bargaining power in the economy.

We can't substantially change opportunity without changing the actual living circumstances of disadvantaged and working-class youth. Therefore, reducing income inequality is essential for improving upward mobility. Here's why:

First, income inequality and intergenerational mobility are closely linked. The so-called Great Gatsby Curve comparing opportunity with equality shows that mobility is less in countries with the greatest inequality. We won't be able to foster more opportunity and mobility without also addressing income inequality.

Second, success in school depends heavily on a child's environment. Policies to increase mobility usually focus on more and better education, including starting earlier and extending schooling through community college or a four-year degree. Yet one of the most robust and long-standing social science research findings is that family background—the circumstances in which children grow up—greatly shapes educational advancement. For example, test score gaps between rich and poor children essentially peak in kindergarten, meaning that family circumstances cement pre-existing inequalities for too many children.

Promoting education solutions to mobility without addressing income inequality is ultimately playing pretend. We can't substantially change opportunity without changing the actual living circumstances of disadvantaged and working-class youth.

Success in school is not as easy for someone facing poverty, especially the concentrated poverty that racial segregation produces. Children from families struggling to make ends meet face a litany of obstacles: They frequently change schools due to poor housing and often have little support in doing their homework. Living in a chaotic and frequently unsafe environment—with parents who are under great stress—they suffer more exposure to lead and asbestos, and endure untreated health problems. For these kids, opportunity is not enough.

If we're serious about reducing inequality, we need to help people earn the kind of living that enables them to provide for their families and build a better future. Without that, promoting mobility and opportunity through more and better education is simply posturing.

> "Societies with pronounced economic inequality suffer from lower long-term GDP growth rates, higher crime rates, poorer public health, increased political inequality, and lower average education levels."

Inequality's Disadvantages Outweigh Its Advantages

Nicholas Birdsong

In the following viewpoint, Nicholas Birdsong identifies the advantages and disadvantages of high-income inequality in a country. He argues that income inequality can drive economic growth and is considered more just to those who invest in an economy. He further contends that inequality can also stifle growth, increase crime, and decrease health for citizens. Birdsong is the faculty services senior researcher at the University of Kansas law library.

"The Consequences of Economic Inequality," Seven Pillars Institute, Nicholas Birdsong, February 5, 2015. Reprinted by permission.

As you read, consider the following questions:

1. What examples does the author give to support his claim that inequality can drive economic growth?
2. According to the author, how does economic inequality impact the social welfare of disadvantaged populations?
3. Why does the author believe that the disadvantages of economic inequality outweigh the advantages?

E conomic inequality" generally refers to the disparity of wealth or income between different groups or within a society. Often characterized by the aphorism "the rich get richer while the poor get poorer," the phrase often refers more specifically to the gap in income or assets between the poorest and richest segments of an individual nation.[1]

Even though the basic concept has entered the public consciousness, the effects of highly concentrated wealth are hotly debated and poorly understood by observers. Research attributes advantages and disadvantages to pronounced levels of economic inequality. Some on the right claim income inequality is socially beneficial in the main despite possible negative effects.

Global trends have led to an increasing concentration of wealth in an increasingly small number of hands. Although some methods of calculating global economic inequality show little change in wealth distribution,[2] different methods of calculating income or wealth tend to come up with different results.[3] The majority of

1 Eduardo Porter, *Why Voters Aren't Angrier About Economic Inequality*, The New York Times, July 24, 2014, http://www.nytimes.com/2014/07/25/upshot/why-voters-arent-angrier-about-economic-inequality.html.
2 Christoph Lakner & Branko Milanovic, *Global Income Distribution*, The World Bank, Dec. 2013, http://www-wds.worldbank.org/external/default/WDSContentServer/IW3P/IB/2013/12/11/000158349_20131211100152/Rendered/PDF/WPS6719.pdf; *Income Inequality Is Not Rising Globally. It's Falling*, The New York Times, July 19, 2014, http://www.nytimes.com/2014/07/20/upshot/income-inequality-is-not-rising-globally-its-falling-.html.
3 Shlomo Yitzhaki, *More than a Dozen Alternative Ways of Spelling Gini*, Hebrew University, Apr. 1, 1997, http://siteresources.worldbank.org/INTDECINEQ/Resources/morethan2002.pdf.

analysts conclude inequality is increasing.[4] In 2013, nearly half of all global wealth was owned by one percent of the global population.[5] On current trends Oxfam says, in its latest research, it expects the wealthiest 1 percent to own more than 50 percent of the world's wealth by 2016. Intra-national inequality has captured the attention of political, business and academic leadership in wealthy nations such as the United States,[6] Japan,[7] and Europe.[8]

The purported consequences of the rich-poor divide are exceedingly diverse. Some economists conclude inequality is beneficial overall for stimulating growth, improves the quality of life for all members of a society, or is merely a necessary part of social progress. Other economists claim wealth concentrations create perpetually oppressed minorities, exploit disadvantaged populations, hinder economic growth, and lead to numerous social problems.

The Benefits of Economic Inequality

Inequality Drives Growth

Rising levels of economic inequality often correlate with economic growth. In 1979, the Chinese government introduced several new

4 Isabel Ortiz & Matthew Cummins, *Global Inequality: Beyond the Bottom Billion*, UNICEF, April 2011, http://www.unicef.org/socialpolicy/files/Global_Inequality.pdf; Graeme Wearden, *Oxfam: 85 richest people as wealthy as poorest half of the world*, The Guardian, Jan. 20, 2014, http://www.theguardian.com/business/2014/jan/20/oxfam -85-richest-people-half-of-the-world; Chad Stone, Danilo Trisi, & Arloc Sherman, *Guide to Statistics on Historical Trends in Income Inequality*, Cntr on Budget and Policy Priorities, Apr. 17, 2014, http://www.cbpp.org/files/11-28-11pov.pdf.

5 *Working for the Few*, 178 Oxfam, 2, Jan. 20, 2014, http://www.oxfam.org/sites/www .oxfam.org/files/bp-working-for-few-political-capture-economic-inequality-200114-en .pdf.

6 *Remarks by the President on Economic Mobility*, The White House, Office of the Press Secretary, Dec. 4, 2013, http://www.whitehouse.gov/the-press-office/2013/12/04/remarks -president-economic-mobility.

7 *The risking sun leaves some Japanese in the shade*, The Economist, June 15, 2006, http:// www.economist.com/node/7066297.

8 John Weeks, *Hobbes, Nobel Prize Winners and Inequality*, The Huffington Post, July 30, 2014, http://www.huffingtonpost.com/johnweeks/hobbes-not-the-stuffed ti_b_5634519 .html.

programs designed to stimulate the economy.[9] Soon afterward, the Chinese GDP annual growth rate rapidly increased from 5.3% in 1979 to over 15% in 1984.[10] The growth rate rose and fell in the years that followed, but China has generally maintained one of the highest rates of growth globally since the 1980's.[11] During the same period of time that rapid Chinese economic growth took place, economic inequality in China also increased noticeably. Currently, China has one of the highest wealth disparities on the planet.[12]

Another example that demonstrates the apparent correlation between economic growth and wealth disparity is the economic expansion the United States experienced in the years prior to 2008. This period coincided with increasing rates of income inequality.[13] Inequality fell between 2007-2008, during the economic recession.[14] Then, as the U.S. economy recovered from the recession, so did rates of income inequality.[15]

Some observers claim the correlation provides evidence economic inequality drives growth in a variety of ways. First, incentives are greater for innovation and entrepreneurship when inequality is pronounced.[16] Large salaried executive positions, for example, create an incentive for lower paid workers to win coveted labor positions.[17] The less-wealthy members of a society work

9 *China GDP: how it has changed since 1980,* The Guardian, March 23, 2012, http://www .theguardian.com/news/datablog/2012/mar/23/china-gdp-since-1980.

10 *Id.*

11 Charles Kenny, *Won't Be Scary Unless They Slow Down,* Bloomberg, July 21, 2014, http://www.businessweek.com/articles/2014-07-21/brics-summit-a-show-of-economic -might-is-nothing-to-fear.

12 Yu Xie & Xiang Zhou, *Income inequality in today's China,* PNAS, Feb. 20, 2014, http:// www.pnas.org/content/early/2014/04/24/1403158111.abstract.

13 *Income Inequality and the Great Recession,* U.S. Congress Joint Economic Committee, 2 (Sept. 2010), http://www.jec.senate.gov/public/?a=Files.Serve&File_id=91975589-257c -403b-8093-8f3b584a088c.

14 *Id.*

15 *Id.*

16 Jonathan D. Ostry, Andrew Berg, & Charalambos G. Tsangarides, *Redistribution, Inequality, and Growth,* Int'l Monetary Fund, April 2014, http://www.imf.org/external/ pubs/ft/sdn/2014/sdn1402.pdf.

17 Example from Edward P. Lazear & Sherwin Rosen, *Rank-Order Tournaments as Optimum Labor Contracts,* 89 The Journal of Political Economy 841 (Oct. 1981), http:// www.jstor.org/stable/1830810.

harder, create new businesses, or invent new products to become a member of the highest income group. On the other hand, when the gap between income levels is small, those in lower income groups have less of an incentive to move up in income.

Some economists argue therefore, that wealth disparities are an inevitable part of a successful economy. Kaldor maintains that long-term market patterns show pulls toward the concentration of wealth.[18] He shows how, in the short term, where inequality is at a minimum, relatively low levels of investment result in lower profit margins, lower consumption levels, lower employment, and lower total income.[19] Subsequently the market demands higher levels of investment and innovation. These increased levels of demand for investment and the trend of technological progress require deep pools of capital to develop innovations and inventions.[20] The process of development and the demand for investment lead to increasing concentration of capital.[21] The concentration of wealth thus results in increasing division between the poor or middle-classes and the wealthy investment class.

Inequality Increases Fairness

Some argue a society with pronounced economic inequality is fairer than a society with a generally equal wealth distribution. Unconstrained markets tend to naturally develop pronounced economic inequalities, as discussed above. Economic equality then generally requires the utilization of redistributive state policies such as progressive taxes. In basic terms, economic equality requires taking from the "have's" and giving to the "have not's."

The idea that property rights should be relatively inviolate forms, in part, the basis for neoliberal economic theory.[22] The state is viewed as a sort of necessary evil for facilitating a free and

---

18 Nicholas Kaldor, *A Model of Economic Growth*, 67 The Economic Journal 591, 622 (Dec. 1957), http://www.jstor.org/stable/2227704.

19 *Id.*

20 *Id.* at 623.

21 *Id.*

22 Ioannis Glinavos, *Neoliberal Law: unintended consequences of market-friendly law reforms*, 29 Third World Quarterly 1087, 1089 (2008).

rationally operating market. Political interference with natural economic processes, such as economic inequality, should be kept to a minimum because substantial government involvement disrupts the moral rights of independence and individual freedom.[23]

Redistribution does not appear fair to some, especially from the perspective of the wealthy. Taxes and other redistributive policies that aim to reduce income inequality involuntarily take assets from individuals without equivalent exchange. Although redistributive policies generally benefit all members of a society, the majority of the costs for those social benefits are borne by the wealthy segments of society.

The Disadvantages of Economic Inequality

Inequality Stifles Growth

A degree of inequality can act as a positive influence on economic growth in the short term.[24] However, some economists find empirical evidence of a negative correlation of about 0.5-0.8 percentage points between long-term growth rates and sustained economic inequality.[25]

A variety of explanations have been proposed to explain how inequality can work to stifle growth. A high level of economic inequality means a higher level of poverty. Poverty is associated with increased crime and poor public health, which places burdens on the economy. In the face of increasing food prices and lower incomes, support for pro-growth government policies declines.[26] Wealthy citizens maintain disproportionate political power compared to poorer citizens,[27] which encourages the development of inefficient tax structures skewed in favor of the wealthy. Unequal

23 *Id.*
24 *See supra* at p. 3.
25 Erik Thorbecke & Chutatong Charumilind, *Economic Inequality and Its Socioeconomic Impact*, 30 World Development 1477, 1482 (April 22, 2002).
26 *Income Inequalities in the Age of Financial Globalization*, Int'l Inst. For Labour Studies, 2 (2008), http://www.ilo.org/wcmsp5/groups/public/—dgreports/—dcomm/—publ/documents/publication/wcms_100354.pdf.
27 *See infra* p. 10.

income distribution increases political instability, which threatens property rights, increases the risk of state repudiated contracts, and discourages capital accumulation.[28] A widening rich-poor gap tends to increase the rate of rent-seeking and predatory market behaviors that hinder economic growth.[29]

According to one theory, growth is suppressed in economically unequal societies, after a phase of increased growth, by the decreasing availability of investments for human capital. Physical capital becomes increasingly scarce, as fewer individuals have funds to invest in training and education.[30] As a result, demands for human capital are difficult or impossible to meet, and economic growth stalls.[31] As an additional consequence, market demands increase for risky unsecured loans, which increase lenders' risk exposure to the borrower's default. More risks in the markets increase market volatility and the possibility of cascading defaults such as the 2008 subprime mortgage crisis.[32]

Inequality Increases Crime

Studies establish a positive relationship between income inequality and crime. According to a survey of research conducted between 1968 and 2000, most researchers point to evidence economically unequal societies have higher crime rates.[33] That survey concludes that inequality is "the single factor most closely and consistently related to crime."[34]

Researchers propose several possible explanations for the inequality-crime correlation. First, disadvantaged members

28 Erik Thorbecke & Chutatong Charumilind, *Economic Inequality and Its Socioeconomic Impact*, 30 World Development 1477, 1484 (April 22, 2002).

29 *Id.*

30 *Id.* at 1483.

31 *Id.*

32 *See* Steve Denning, *Lest We Forget: Why We Had A Financial Crisis*, Forbes, Nov. 22, 2011, http://www.forbes.com/sites/stevedenning/2011/11/22/5086/; Ian Katz & Simon Kennedy, *Geithner Urges End to European 'Cascading Default' Threat*, Bloomberg, Sept. 24, 2011, http://www.businessweek.com/news/2011-09-24/geithner-urges-end-to-european -cascading-default-threat.html.

33 *Id.* at 160.

34 *Id.* at 178.

of a society may be more likely to suffer from resentment and hostility as a result of their economic position or competition over scarce jobs or resources, resulting in a higher propensity for criminal behavior.[35]

Second, inequality increases the incentive to commit crimes. Fewer methods of lawfully obtaining resources are available for the increasing number of poor who live in an unequal society. Even when risks of punishments are taken into account, illegal methods of gaining assets may provide better returns than legal means of obtaining resources.[36]

Third, a wide gap between rich and poor tends to increase crime by reducing law enforcement spending in low-income areas. Wealthy members of a society tend to concentrate in secluded communities, especially as the disparity between the rich and poor increase.[37] Rich neighborhoods or countries have more funds for the police than their poorer counterparts, resulting in a less effective police force or a higher number of officers susceptible to bribes in an increasing number of poor areas. Increasingly concentrated wealth leads to higher crime rates in poor areas which are prevalent in economically unbalanced societies. In societies with a sufficiently high degree of economic inequality, state investments in reducing economic inequality is vastly more effective at reducing crime than increasing spending law enforcement.[38]

35 Lisa Stolzenberg, David Eitle, Stewart J. D'Alessio, *Race, economic inequality, and violent crime*, 34 Journal of Criminal Justice 303, 303 (2006).

36 *Income Inequalities in the Age of Financial Globalization*, Int'l Inst. For Labour Studies, p. 11 (2008), http://www.ilo.org/wcmsp5/groups/public/—dgreports/—dcomm/—publ/documents/publication/wcms_100354.pdf.

37 Richard Fry & Paul Taylor, *The Rise of Residential Segregation by Income*, Aug. 1, 2012, Pew Research, http://www.pewsocialtrends.org/2012/08/01/the-rise-of-residential-segregation-by-income/.

38 Bardhan, Bowles, & Wallerstein, *Globalization and egalitarian redistribution*, Princeton University Press (2006).

Inequality Decreases Health

The impoverished members of society are subject to disproportionate occurrence rates of certain kinds of illnesses. Access to quality health care and healthy food is sometimes limited or unavailable for poor individuals. The result of a substantial poor population, a defining feature of economic inequality, is a less effective lower-income work force, higher disease and mortality rates, higher health care costs, and progressively deepening poverty for afflicted groups.

Food deserts are a unique characteristic of economically unequal societies, characterized by the lack of readily accessible healthy and affordable food. Food deserts occur in several heavily industrialized Western nations, including the United Kingdom, Canada, Australia and New Zealand.[39] The term "food desert" originated in Scotland during the early 1990s in the context of a public sector housing report.[40] Although the term originated in Scotland, its prevalence steadily increased since the 1990s in the United Kingdom, eventually becoming a common topic of research affecting public policy internationally.[41] In 2009, 2.2 percent of all households in the United States were located in food deserts.[42] In the United States and other industrialized Western nations, the lack of access to fresh foods is associated with disproportionate obesity and diet-related disease rates among low-income households.

There is an growing interest in food deserts as obesity rates and other diet-related illnesses increase. Obesity rates in the United

39 Julie Beaulac, Elizabeth Krisjansson, & Steven Cummins, *A Systematic Review of Food Deserts, 1966-2007*, Preventing Chronic Disease, July 2009, http://www.cdc.gov/pcd/issues/2009/jul/08_0163.htm.

40 Steven Cummins & Sally Macintyre, *"Food deserts" – evidence and assumption in health policy making*, 325 BMJ 436, http://www.ncbi.nlm.nih.gov/pmc/articles/PMC1123946/pdf/436.pdf.

41 Julie Beaulac, Elizabeth Krisjansson, & Steven Cummins, *A Systematic Review of Food Deserts, 1966-2007*, Preventing Chronic Disease, July 2009, http://www.cdc.gov/pcd/issues/2009/jul/08_0163.htm.

42 Michele Ver Ploeg, et al. *Access to Affordable and Nutritious Food – Measuring and Understanding Food Deserts and Their Consequences: Report to Congress*, USDA, June 2009, http://www.ers.usda.gov/publications/ap-administrative-publication/ap-036.aspx#.U0IMDa1dWEw.

States began to increase at alarming rates during the late 1970s and early 1980s. Currently, more than 1 in 3 American adults are obese and 2 out of 3 are overweight or obese.[43] Increases in the number of new diabetes diagnoses accompany the trend of increasing weight. The number of individuals suffering from high cholesterol has decreased, although the trend may be attributed to increasing consumption of cholesterol-lowering medications.[44] Health care costs in the United States were $75 billion in 1970, $2.6 trillion in 2010, and are expected to reach $4.8 trillion in 2021.[45] While not attributed solely to diet, unhealthy lifestyles account for a substantial portion of the rising expenditures on health care.[46] Obesity increases health care costs by $147 billion every year in the United States, or $1,429 more per person than a normally weighted person.[47] Obesity and diet-related diseases contribute to about 10 percent of all health care costs in the United States.[48] Poor diets are a cause of conditions such as diabetes, heart disease, osteoarthritis, some cancers, and other diseases.[49]

Impoverished Americans have been especially affected by the nation's deteriorating average quality of health. Americans living in the poorest neighborhoods are more likely to be obese than Americans living above the poverty line.[50] Additionally, individuals

43 *Adult Obesity Facts*, CDC (*last accessed* Apr. 6, 2014), http://www.cdc.gov/obesity/data/adult.html.
44 *See* Elena V. Kuklina; Margaret D. Carroll; Kate M. Shaw; Rosemarie Hirsch,*Trends in High LDL Cholesterol, Cholesterol-lowering Medication Use, and Dietary Saturated-fat Intake: United States, 1976-2010*, CDC, Mar. 2013, http://www.cdc.gov/nchs/data/databriefs/db117.htm.
45 *The Facts About Rising Health Care Costs*, Aetna (last accessed Apr. 14, 2014), http://www.aetna.com/health-reform-connection/aetnas-vision/facts-about-costs.html.
46 *Id.*
47 *Adult Obesity Facts*, CDC (*last accessed* Apr. 6, 2014), http://www.cdc.gov/obesity/data/adult.html.
48 Eric A. Finkelstein et al., *Annual Medical Spending Attributable To Obesity: Payer-And Service-Specific Estimates*, 5 Health Affairs 822 (July 27, 2009), http://content.healthaffairs.org/content/28/5/w822.full.pdf+html.
49 *Economic Costs*, Harvard School of Pub. Health (*last accessed* Apr. 6, 2014), http://www.hsph.harvard.edu/obesity-prevention-source/obesity-consequences/economic/.
50 James A. Levine, *Poverty and Obesity in the U.S.*, American Diabetes Ass'n, Nov. 2011, http://diabetes.diabetesjournals.org/content/60/11/2667.full.

living below the federal poverty level are two times more likely to die from diabetes.[51]

Considerable inconvenience and time constraints create barriers to cheap groceries for citizens living in food deserts. The incentive is increased for residents to purchase processed sugary and fatty items from gas stations, convenience stores, fast food restaurants, or other sources of unhealthy food.[52] Residents who are elderly, disabled, or have children are often less mobile, and the incentive to rely on convenient yet unhealthy foods is even greater. As a result, residents living in the food desert are more prone to obesity and other diet related diseases.

Beyond the direct health care costs of food deserts, poor health impacts the prosperity of a society. Poor health forces communities to cope with a less effective workforce, higher mortality rates, higher life insurance premiums, and a less prosperous economy.[53] A poorer economy may result in fewer taxable resources, and subsequently either higher overall tax rates or inferior public services. Food deserts also reinforce wealth disparities. Lower-income persons live in food deserts and face higher costs as a result. The poor are disproportionately burdened with higher health care costs, a disadvantaged ability to work, and a higher percentage of time spent on obtaining food.

Economic Inequality Increases Political Inequality

When wealth distribution becomes concentrated in a small number of hands, political power tends to become skewed in favor of that small wealthy group. High-income groups are able and incentivized to manipulate government in their favor through both legal processes and through corrupt practices. Impoverished or working class groups are simultaneously less able to become

51 Sharon Saydah & Kimberly Lochner, *Socioeconomic Status and Risk of Diabetes-Related Mortality in the U.S.*, 125 Pub. Health Rep. 377 (2010), May-Jun, http://www.ncbi.nlm.nih .gov/pmc/articles/PMC2848262/.
52 *USDA Defines Food Deserts*, Am. Nutrition Ass'n (*last accessed* Apr. 6, 2014), http:// americannutritionassociation.org/newsletter/usda-defines-food-deserts.
53 *Id.*

educated or participate in the political process as economic means become increasingly scarce.

Wealthy groups receive political advantages in several different ways. In democratic societies that lack public financing of campaigns such as the United States, political figures require private financial backing in order to run effective campaigns. Federal candidates during the 2010 elections cycle spent around six billion dollars altogether.[54] Successful candidates in Senate races spent an average of $10.3 million on their elections, while winning Congressional candidates spent an average of $1.6 million.[55] While more money spent does not always result in more votes, campaign expenditures correlate so closely with votes that researchers have been able to reliably predict that for every $5 spent, a candidate will receive approximately one vote.[56]

Political figures are required to court potential wealthy donors in order to fund successful campaigns. Half or more of the average Congressperson's time is spent speaking with potential donors and raising money.[57] According to one report, "It is considered poor form in Congress—borderline self-indulgent—for a freshman [legislator] to sit at length in congressional hearings when the time could instead be spent raising money."[58] Wealthy donors are given extreme access to elected officials. Politicians are likely to be reluctant to support policies that are not in the interests of their wealthy backers for fear of loosing vital financial support and subsequently the next election.

Low-income groups are less able to influence elected officials. Political interest and involvement is substantially depressed in economically unequal societies. According to one survey,

---

54 *Naming names; Campaign finance,* Nov. 24, 2012, The Economist (London).
55 Paul Steinhauser & Robert Yoon, *Cost to win congressional election skyrockets,* CNN, July 11, 2013, http://www.cnn.com/2013/07/11/politics/congress-election-costs/.
56 Philip Bump, *Does More Campaign Money Actually Buy More Votes: An Investigation,* The Wire, Nov. 11, 2013.
57 Ryan Grim & Sabrina Sidiqui, *Call Time for Congress Shows How Fundraising Dominates Bleak Work Life,* The Huffington Post, Jan. 8, 2013, http://www.huffingtonpost.com/2013/01/08/call-time-congressional-fundraising_n_2427291.html.
58 *Id.*

individuals living in the most economically equal societies are four times more likely to be actively involved in politics and 2.7 times more likely to vote compared to the most economically unequal society.[59] Poorer groups are politically disadvantaged by the inability to dedicate time for political activities. Lower income groups tend to spend more time at work or securing basic needs. Consequently, they are less able to invest time or money to obtain political knowledge or participate in the political process. Additionally, economic inequality decreases participation by the poor because the poor are less able to influence outcomes.[60] The apparent futility of low-income groups' efforts to influence policy discourages subsequent attempts to affect policies.

Wealth concentration further concentrates political power by the increased ability of wealthy groups to corrupt political processes. Some government officials may be especially susceptible to bribes if the officials are subject to the increased economic pressures present in an economically unequal society. Further, extremely wealthy community members are more able to afford to pay bribes in a relatively unequal economic state.

Inequality Decreases Education

Substantial empirical research reveal link education and poverty. Nations with a high degree of economic equality and a relatively small low-income population tend to have a substantially higher level of education.[61] A one-point increase in the Gini coefficient (a measurement of income inequality) translates into a 10% decrease in high school graduation rates and a 40% increase in college graduation.[62] In an economically unequal society, the society-wide average level of education decreases while the number of educational elites increases.

---

59 Frederick Solt, *Economic inequality and democratic political engagement*, 52 American Journal of Political Science, 48 (2008).
60 *Id.* at 49.
61 Erik Thorbecke & Chutatong Charumilind, *Economic Inequality and Its Socioeconomic Impact*, 30 World Development 1477, 1488 (April 22, 2002).
62 *Id.*

One proposed causal connection between education and inequality is unequal societies tend to underinvest in education. Absent private or public scholarship programs, the poor are unable to afford to pay for education or spend the time in school that could have otherwise been spent working. Sweatshops in countries like Bangladesh provide an example of poverty's effect on education. Sweatshops in Bangladesh employ young children, which give destitute families much needed economic support.[63] However, the children who work in the sweatshops are unable to attend schools or obtain an education because of their economic needs. The children's future earning potential decline and the likelihood increases the child and the family continue to live in poverty.[64]

In unequal societies, government support tends to decline for public education programs. As the rich become increasingly wealthy, public policies become increasingly favorable to the policy goals of the economic elites.[65] Public education programs tend to be unpopular with the wealthy because they involve taking public funds, which often primarily consist of taxes imposed on the rich, and redistributing those resources to the poor.[66]

The beneficial effect of increased GDP growth correlates with higher rates of inequality. From the perspective of the wealthy or liberal economic theorists, fairness is maximized in economically stratified societies that avoid redistributive policies. However, the disadvantages of economic inequality are more numerous and arguably more significant than the benefits. Societies with pronounced economic inequality suffer from lower long-term GDP growth rates, higher crime rates, poorer public health, increased political inequality, and lower average education levels.

---

63 Benjamin Powell, *Sweatshops In Bangladesh Improve The Lives of Their Workers, and Boost Growth*, Forbes (May 2, 2013), http://www.forbes.com/sites/realspin/2013/05/02/sweatshops-in-bangladesh-improve-the-lives-of-their-workers-and-boost-growth/.
64 *See supra* note 61 (empirical data showing that educated societies tend to have more equal income distribution).
65 *See supra* page 10.
66 *See supra* page 5.

> "*Capitalist culture engenders a mindset among politicians that leads them to craft public policies in favor of … the rich and powerful, and turn their backs on the poor*"

Capitalism Causes a Wealth Gap

Ann Robertson and Bill Leumer

In the following viewpoint, Ann Robertson and Bill Leumer argue that the inherent tendency in capitalism to maximize profits while minimizing the costs of labor results in the growth of economic inequality in a society. The authors contend that wealthy capitalists influence government policy makers to create advantageous policies that encourage inequality. They predict that eventually the working class will grow tired of being exploited and exert power to improve their conditions. Robertson is a lecturer at San Francisco State University and a member of the California Faculty Association. Leumer is a member of the International Brotherhood of Teamsters, Local 853 (ret.).

"Does Capitalism Inevitably Produce Inequalities?" Ann Robertson and Bill Leumer, Common Dreams, July 2, 2014. http://www.commondreams.org/views/2014/07/02/does-capitalism-inevitably-produce-inequalities. Licensed under CC BY-SA 3.0.

As you read, consider the following questions:

1. What role do the authors believe that capitalism has played in increasing the wealth gap?
2. According to the authors, how has the ratio of CEO pay to worker pay changed in the last forty-five years?
3. How do the authors describe the culture and worldview of wealthy capitalists and policy makers?

I n a recent New York Times op-ed article, Nobel Prize-winning economist Joseph Stiglitz theorized that capitalism does not inevitably produce inequalities in wealth. Instead, he argued, today's inequalities result from policy decisions made by politicians on all sorts of matters that affect people's income: the tax structure that favors the rich, the bailout of the banks during the Great Recession, subsidies for rich farmers, cutting of food stamps, etc. In fact, he concluded, today there are no "truly fundamental laws of capitalism." Thanks to democracy, people can steer the economy in a variety of directions and no single outcome is inevitable.

In their 2010 book, "Winner-Take-All Politics: How Washington Made the Rich Richer—and Turned Its Back on the Middle Class," Yale Professor Jacob Hacker and U.C. Berkeley Professor Paul Pierson would seem to add additional support to Stiglitz's conclusion. As reported by Bob Herbert in The New York Times, they argued that "the economic struggles of the middle and working classes in the U.S. since the late-1970s were not primarily the result of globalization and technological changes but rather a long series of policy changes in government that overwhelmingly favored the rich."

Although there is certainly significant substance to Stiglitz's argument—policy decisions can have profound impacts on economic outcomes—nevertheless capitalism is far more responsible for economic inequality because of its inherent nature and its extended reach in the area of policy decisions than Stiglitz is willing to concede.

To begin with, in capitalist society it is much easier to make money if you already have money, and much more difficult if you are poor. So, for example, a rich person can buy up a number of foreclosed houses and rent them out to desperate tenants at ridiculously high rates. Then, each time rent is paid, the landlord becomes richer and the tenant becomes poorer, and inequalities in wealth grow.

More importantly, at the very heart of capitalism lies an incentive that leads to the increase of inequalities. Capitalism is based on the principle of competition, and businesses must compete with one another in order to survive. Each company, therefore, strives to maximize its profits in order to achieve a competitive advantage. For example, they can use extra profits to offset lowering the price of their product, undersell their opponents, and push them out of the market.

But in order to maximize profits, businesses must keep productive costs to a minimum. And a major portion of productive costs includes labor. Consequently, as a general rule, in order for a business to survive, it must push labor costs to a minimum. And that is why, of course, so many businesses migrate from the U.S. and relocate in countries like China, Viet Nam, Mexico, and Bangladesh where wages are a mere pittance.

This inherent tendency to maximize profits while minimizing the cost of labor directly results in growing inequalities. Stiglitz himself mentions that C.E.O's today "enjoy incomes that are on average 295 times that of the typical worker, a much higher ratio than in the past." In fact, in 1970, the ratio was roughly 40 times. C.E.O.s who succeed in suppressing wages are routinely rewarded for their efforts. Hence, not only is there an incentive to keep wages low for the survival of the business, there is a personal incentive in play as well.

While Stiglitz is correct in arguing that politicians can influence economic outcomes by policy decisions, what he fails to acknowledge is that these policy decisions themselves are heavily influenced by the economic relations established by capitalism.

There is no firewall between the economy and politics. Those who have acquired money from the economic sector can then put this money to work in the political sector by lobbying and showering politicians with campaign contributions. Although politicians religiously deny that these contributions have any influence on their decisions, it is inconceivable that businesses—always obsessed with their "bottom line"—would continue these contributions without a "return on their investment."

Study after study has confirmed the influence of money on political decisions. The San Francisco Chronicle reported, for example: "In a state with nearly 38 million people, few have more influence than the top 100 donors to California campaigns—a powerful club that has contributed overwhelmingly to Democrats and spent $1.25 billion to influence voters over the past dozen years. These big spenders represent a tiny fraction of the hundreds of thousands of individuals and groups that donated to California campaigns from 2001 through 2011. But they supplied about one-third of the $3.67 billion given to state campaigns during that time, campaign records show. With a few exceptions, these campaign elites have gotten their money's worth, according to California Watch's analysis of campaign data from state finance records and the nonpartisan National Institute on Money in State Politics, which tracks the influence of campaign money on state elections."

Even beyond campaign contributions, political decisions are not crafted in a vacuum, remote from capitalism. Capitalism is a way of life, and for that reason it generates its own peculiar culture and world view that envelopes every other social sphere, a culture that includes competition, individualism, materialism in the form of consumerism, operating in one's self-interest without consideration for the needs of others, and so on. This culture infects everyone to one degree or another; it is like an ether that all those in its proximity inhale. It encourages people to evaluate one another according to their degree of wealth and power. It rewards those who doggedly pursue their narrow self-interests at the expense of others.

The culture of capitalism, because of its hyper individualism, also produces an extraordinarily narrow vision of the world. Viewing the world from an isolated standpoint, individuals tend to assume that they are self-made persons, not the products of their surrounding culture and social relations. So the rich assume that their wealth has been acquired through their personal talents alone, while they see those mired in poverty as lacking the ambition and willingness to work hard. People are unable to see the complexities underlying human behavior because of the atomization of social life. But the disciplines of psychology, sociology, and anthropology all concur that individuals are overwhelmingly a product of their social environment to their very core.

In 1947, for example, the American Anthropological Association argued in its Statement on Human Rights: "If we begin, as we must, with the individual, we find that from the moment of his birth not only his behavior, but his very thought, his hopes, aspirations, the moral values which direct his action and justify and give meaning to his life in his own eyes and those of his fellow, are shaped by the body of custom of the group of which he becomes a member."

It is in this more subtle way that capitalism induces growing income inequalities. Because of their intensely competitive environment, politicians are more vulnerable to this capitalist culture than most. Capitalist culture engenders a mindset among politicians that leads them to craft public policies in favor of the good people, the rich and powerful, and turn their backs on the poor or punish them with mass incarceration. They think it entirely natural to accept money from the wealthy in order to fund their re-election campaigns. And the more the inequalities in wealth grow, the more this mindset blinds politicians to the destructive implications of these "natural" decisions.

In 2011, Stiglitz wrote a compelling article, "Of the 1%, by the 1%, for the 1%," in which he argued forcefully that large inequalities in wealth are in no one's interest. But since then the politicians have continued to accept campaign contributions from the rich, socialize with them, and do their bidding. They ritually denounce the shamelessly low taxes on the 1%, but have done nothing to alter them. The culture of capitalism trumps logical arguments, and thus the inequalities in wealth continue to expand. Capitalism has an iron grip on the political process.

Stiglitz concluded his article with this prophetic statement: "The top 1 percent have the best houses, the best educations, the best doctors, and the best lifestyles, but there is one thing that money doesn't seem to have bought: an understanding that their fate is bound up with how the other 99 percent live. Throughout history, this is something that the top 1 percent eventually do learn. Too late."

While Stiglitz's arguments have had no impact on growing inequalities, thanks to the power of capitalism, nevertheless capitalism gets credit for producing the one force that can put a stop to these destructive trends: the working class. As Karl Marx argued, capitalism produces its own "gravediggers." In the 1930s workers massively organized unions and fought militant battles to defend their right to unionize and their right to fair compensation. These unions, which Stiglitz fails to mention, played a decisive role in reining in inequalities and unleashing a period in which the ranks of "the middle class" grew.

As Marx noted in his "Contribution to a Critique of Hegel's Philosophy of Right," "The weapon of criticism cannot, of course, replace criticism of the weapon, material force must be overthrown by material force; but theory also becomes a material force as soon as it has gripped the masses."

Stiglitz's criticisms of growing inequality will have little impact on policy decisions until they are embraced by the masses, the working class, those that capitalism cruelly exploits and who are so easily dismissed by politicians and academics. At that point the working class will finally stand up and collectively declare enough is enough.

> *"Keeping wealth in the hands of the wealthy is wiser than giving it to the government."*

America Benefits from Income Inequality

Jennifer Larino

In the following viewpoint, Jennifer Larino describes the economic philosophy of author John Tamny, who argues that income inequality has been a positive driving force of American innovation. Tamny uses former Apple CEO Steve Jobs as an example of someone who became a billionaire by providing an innovation that benefits everyone. Tamny believes that wealthy people create jobs, invest to help businesses grow, and provide funds for banks to lend. Larino is a reporter for the New Orleans Times-Picayune.

As you read, consider the following questions:

1. Why does John Tamny believe that without income inequality, Americans would be worse off?
2. According to Tamny, how have technology billionaires benefited society?
3. According to Tamny, what options do wealthy people have for using their money?

I ncome inequality—and how to solve it—is shaping up to be a rallying topic as candidates rev up bids for the 2016 presidential race. But is income inequality truly a problem?

John Tamny, a political economy editor at Forbes and author, doesn't think so.

Tamny argues the disparity between the wealthy and the poor has been a driving force in American innovation in his latest book "Popular Economics: What the Rolling Stones, Downton Abbey, and LeBron James Can Teach You About Economics."

Without income inequality, Tamny says, we would all be worse off.

Tamny is in New Orleans Tuesday evening (April 21) to talk about income inequality and the economic role it plays at a talk sponsored by Metairie Park Country Day School and Isidore Newman School.

The event starts at 6 p.m. in the Henson Auditorium on Newman's Uptown campus. It is free and open to the public.

In an interview Monday with NOLA.com | The Times-Picayune, Tamny pointed to mobile phones as an example of the good that can result from income inequality.

In the 1980s, a mobile phone was a privilege of the very wealthy. It came in a bag and cost more than $2,000, not including exorbitant fees for calls. Today, most people, rich or poor, can afford a mobile phone.

Tamny noted quite a few people got rich—billionaire rich—building out the telecom infrastructure and designing devices that opened access to mobile phone use to the masses.

Apple's Steve Jobs made billions cornering the smartphone market with the iPhone. Apple could have hiked up prices, but it lowered them instead to allow more people to buy the device, Tamny said.

The prospect of making lots of money is what drives ambitious people to dive into new, unknown markets, he said. America should encourage that, not quash it, he added.

AMERICAN PERCEPTIONS OF WEALTH

What do Americans think of the rich? Views are mixed: Americans view the well-to-do as more intelligent and more hardworking but also greedier, our survey this summer found.

About four-in-ten (43%) said the rich were more likely than the average person to be intelligent (with 50% saying there was no difference or expressing no opinion) and 42% said they were more likely to be hardworking compared with 24% who said less likely and 34% seeing no difference or offering no opinion. More than half (55%) saw the rich as more likely to be greedy compared with 9% who said less likely, and 36% who took neither side.

Republicans were more likely to describe the rich as hardworking, by a 55% to 33% margin. About two-thirds (65%) of Democrats saw the rich as greedy compared to 42% of Republicans.

When it comes to the question of why people are poor, less than half (46%) of those surveyed said that circumstances beyond one's control were more often to blame while 38% said an individual's lack of effort was more to blame. About one-in-ten (11%) cited both factors. In addition, 65% believed that most poor people in the U.S. do work but were unable to earn enough money. Just 23% said the poor do not work.

"Americans See Growing Gap Between Rich and Poor," Bruce Drake, December 5, 2013.

"We are a much more unequal society today precisely because people have gotten rich shrinking the lifestyle gap," Tamny said.

After World War II, the income gap between rich and poor actually decreased as America built a middle class on growing demand for factory workers and other low and moderate skill labor.

Over the past three decades, however, the trend has reversed. Top marginal tax rates fell and executive pay rose. Low-skill factory jobs were shipped overseas or automated, removing good-paying jobs for many.

Last year, the richest 1 percent of U.S. adults held about 38.4 percent of the nation's wealth in mid-2014, according to the Credit Suisse Research Institute Global Wealth Report released in October 2014.

Incomes for the wealthy are growing, while everyone else sees stagnant earnings. The disparity has fed calls to raise the minimum wage and increase taxes on the rich among other proposals.

Tamny thinks America should embrace its billionaires, not tax them more.

He noted rich people have options for how they use their money—they can spend it, invest it, give it away or hold onto it.

Spending creates jobs for people who provide those goods and services. Investments in the stock market or private equity allow businesses to grow.

Even the stingiest billionaires keep their money in a bank. The bank pays them interest and uses the money to fund loans to businesses and consumers, Tamny said.

Keeping wealth in the hands of the wealthy is wiser than giving it to the government, Tamny argued.

He noted Isidore Newman School as an example. The private school was founded in 1903 by Isidore Newman, founder of the Maison Blanche department store chain. Newman, a German immigrant, used his wealth to fund philanthropic efforts in New Orleans.

"Market forces are going to dictate where that wealth will go," Tamny said.

Tamny said he does not intend to downplay the battles the poor face every day. But he thinks the push to solve income inequality fails to look at the benefits.

Despite arguments to the contrary, Tamny, a Southern California resident and graduate of the University of Texas at Austin, believes the U.S. still offers the opportunity for all people to make a better life for themselves. There would be no immigration debate if that were not true, he said.

The country benefits from its billionaires as much as the aspiring, ambitious people that drive its economy day in and day out, he said.

"Imagine the world without a Steve Jobs or a Bill Gates," Tamny said. "There would be less inequality but it would be a sad world."

Periodical and Internet Sources Bibliography

The following articles have been selected to supplement the diverse views presented in this chapter.

Surtirtha Bagchi and Jan Svejnar, "Does Wealth Inequality Matter for Growth? The Effect of Billionaire Wealth, Income Distribution, and Poverty," Cato Institute, October 14, 2015.

Markus Brückner and Daniel Lederman, "Effects of Income Inequality on Economic Growth," *VOX*, July 7, 2015.

Era Dabla-Norris, Kalpana Kochhar, Frantisek Ricka, Nujin Suphaphiphat, and Evridiki Tsounta, "Causes and Consequences of Income Inequality: A Global Perspective," International Monetary Fund, June 2015.

Rob Garver, "How Income Inequality Can Hurt the Economy," *The Fiscal Times*, April 22, 2014.

Catharine Bond Hill, "Income Inequality and Higher Education," American Council on Education, Summer 2015.

Tuomas Malinen, "The Economic Consequences of Income Inequality," *Huffington Post*, December 21, 2015.

Eduardo Porter, "Income Equality: A Search for Consequences," *New York Times*, March 25, 2014.

Rebecca Vallas, Christian E. Weller, Rachel West, and Jackie Odum, "The Effect of Rising Inequality on Social Security," Center for American Progress, February 10, 2015.

Igor Volsky, "6 Ways Extreme Income Inequality Is Making Your Life Worse," Think Progress, January 28, 2014.

Ray Williams, "Why Income Inequality Threatens Democracy," *Psychology Today*, August 12, 2015.

For Further Discussion

Chapter 1

1. In what ways do the authors use statistics to analyze the wealth gap and income inequality ?
2. Several of the authors claim that it is impossible to compare the composition of the high-income household to those of middle and lower classes. From your reading of the viewpoints, how are these groups different?
3. Thomas A. Garrett contends that US income inequality "has many economic benefits." How do you think Salvatore Babones would respond to that statement?

Chapter 2

1. Miles Corak claims that income inequality "changes opportunities, incentives and institutions that form, develop and transmit characteristics and skills valued in the labor market." How is that claim illustrated in Edward McClelland's viewpoint?
2. Niall Ferguson tells the story of entrepreneur Elon Musk. Is Musk an example or an exception to the American Dream? Explain your answer.
3. From your reading of the viewpoints in this chapter, do you think Americans have more access to upward mobility that other developed and English-speaking countries? Why or why not?

Chapter 3

1. Several viewpoints in this chapter discuss the merits of redistribution, or taxing the wealthy to provide benefits for the poor. Why does Doug Mataconis think that this is bad policy?
2. Scott Santens proposes a universal flat tax as a way to relieve income inequality. Why do you think so few countries have tried this policy?
3. After reading his viewpoint, why do you think so many young adults supported Bernie Sanders in his run for the candidacy for US president?

Chapter 4

1. Using at least two viewpoints as evidence, make a claim that income inequality either does or does not harm society. Explain your reasoning.
2. Several viewpoints claim that US tax policies favor the wealthy. What suggestions do the authors make to reform the collection and spending of tax revenues?
3. Authors of these viewpoints present several suggestions for government policies to increase economic mobility for lower and middle classes. Which suggestions do you think are likely to be successful and why?

Organizations to Contact

The editors have compiled the following list of organizations concerned with the issues debated in this book. The descriptions are derived from materials provided by the organizations. All have publications or information available for interested readers. The list was compiled on the date of publication of the present volume; the information provided here may change. Be aware that many organizations take several weeks or longer to respond to inquiries, so allow as much time as possible.

American Association of University Women (AAUW)
111 Sixteenth Street NW
Washington, DC 20036
(800) 326-2287
Email: connect@aauw.org
Website: http://www.aauw.org

The American Association of University Women (AAUW) advocates for equity and education for women and girls. AAUW members have examined and taken positions on the educational, social, economic, and political issues that concern girls and women. Its website contains background and explanations on topics such as gender equity, sex discrimination, and educational opportunities for women.

American Enterprise Institute for Public Policy Research (AEI)
1150 Seventeenth Street NW
Washington, DC 20036
(202) 862-5800
Email: info@aei.org
Website: http://www.aei.org

The American Enterprise Institute for Public Policy Research (AEI) is a private, nonpartisan, not-for-profit research organization focusing on defending the principles and improving the institutions of American freedom and democratic capitalism. It provides research and information on a variety of topics, such as the world economy, foreign policy, education, and domestic political and social issues.

American Federation of Labor and Congress of Industrial Organizations (AFL-CIO)
815 Sixteenth Street NW
Washington, DC 20006
(202) 637-5000
Website: http://www.aflcio.org

The American Federation of Labor and Congress of Industrial Organizations (AFL-CIO) is a voluntary federation of fifty-six unions representing 12.5 million working men and women. The AFL-CIO educates union members about issues affecting the daily lives of working families and provides a voice for them in government and business. Its website provides information and reports on topics such as legislation, political action, and workplace rights.

Brookings Institution
1775 Massachusetts Avenue NW
Washington, DC 20036
(202) 797-6000
Email: mailto:communications@brookings.edu
Website: http://www.brookings.edu

The Brookings Institution is a nonprofit organization devoted to independent research and policy solutions. Its mission is to conduct high-quality, independent research and, based on that research, to provide innovative, practical recommendations for policy makers and the public. Resources on economic policies and governance are available on its website.

Cato Institute
1000 Massachusetts Avenue NW
Washington, DC 20001-5403
(202) 842-0200
Website: http://www.cato.org

The Cato Institute is a public policy research organization dedicated to the principles of individual liberty, limited government, free markets, and peace. Its scholars and analysts conduct independent, nonpartisan research on a wide range of policy issues. Its website provides research materials and commentaries on economic policies and government interventions.

Center for American Progress (CAP)
1333 H Street NW, 10th Floor
Washington, DC 20005
(202) 682-1611
Website: http://www.americanprogress.org

The Center for American Progress is an independent, nonpartisan policy institute that is dedicated to improving the lives of Americans through progressive ideas and action. The goals of CAP are to develop new policy ideas, challenge the media to cover the issues that truly matter, and shape the national debate. CAP publishes a newsletter, *InProgress,* as well as reports on a variety of topics, such as the US labor market, poverty, and government policies.

Center for Economic and Policy Research (CEPR)
1611 Connecticut Avenue NW, Suite 400
Washington, DC 20009
(202) 293-5380
Email: info@cepr.net
Website: http://www.cepr.net

The mission of the Center for Economic and Policy Research (CEPR) is to promote democratic debate on the most important economic and social issues that affect people's lives. CEPR conducts both professional research and public education on a variety of economic and public policy issues. Its website provides information and analysis on topics such as trade, tax policy, and government programs.

Center on Budget and Policy Priorities (CBPP)
820 First Street NE, Suite 510
Washington, DC 20002
(202) 408-1080
Email: center @sbpp.org
Website: http://www.cbpp.org

The Center on Budget and Policy Priorities (CBPP) is a nonpartisan research and policy institute. Its mission is to pursue federal and state policies designed both to reduce poverty and inequality and to restore fiscal responsibility in equitable and effective ways. CBPP provides information on budget and tax issues and programs and policies that help low-income people in order to help inform debates and achieve better policy outcomes. Its website provides reports on health reform, tax policies, and poverty programs.

Congressional Budget Office
Ford House Office Building
Second and D Street
Washington, DC 20515-6925
(202) 226-2602
Website: http://www.cbo.gov

Since 1975, CBO has produced independent analyses of budgetary and economic issues to support the Congressional budget process. Each year, the agency's economists and budget analysts produce dozens of reports and hundreds of cost estimates for proposed legislation. CBO is strictly nonpartisan; conducts objective, impartial analysis; and hires its employees solely on the basis of professional competence without regard to political affiliation.

Economic Policy Institute (EPI)
1333 H Street NW, Suite 300, East Tower
Washington, DC 20005-4707
(202) 775-8810
Email: epi@epi.org
Website: http://www.epi.org

The Economic Policy Institute (EPI) is a nonprofit, nonpartisan research organization that focuses on the needs of low- and middle-income workers in economic policy discussions. EPI conducts research and analysis on the economic status of working America. EPI proposes public policies that protect and improve the economic conditions of low- and middle-income workers and assesses policies with respect to how they affect those workers. Its website provides a searchable database of publications on topics such as income inequality, poverty, pay issues, and jobs and unemployment.

Institute for Policy Studies
1301 Connecticut Avenue NW, Suite 600
Washington, DC 20036
(202) 234-9382
Email: info@ips-dc.org
Website: http://www.ips-dc.org

The Institute for Policy Studies is a multi-issue progressive think tank that serves as a resource for policy makers and public scholars. It has provided critical support for major social movements by producing seminal books, films, and articles; educating key policy makers and the general public; and crafting practical strategies in support of peace, justice, and the environment.

Institute for Women's Policy Research (IWPR)
1200 Eighteenth Street NW, Suite 301
Washington, DC 20036
(202) 785-5100
Email: iwpr@iwpr.org
Website: http://www.iwpr.org

The Institute for Women's Policy Research conducts research and disseminates its findings to address the needs of women, promote public dialog, and strengthen families, communities, and societies. IWPR supports initiatives on such topics as pay equity and discrimination, welfare reform, child care, and women's access to health care. Its website provides a searchable database of reports and research summaries on a wide variety of topics relating to women and families.

United for a Fair Economy (UFE)
62 Summer Street
Boston, MA 20110
(617) 423-2148
Email: info@faireconomy.org
Website: http://www.faireconomy.org

United for a Fair Economy (UFE) is a nonpartisan, nonprofit organization whose mission is to raise awareness about income inequality and its impact on American families. It works to educate Americans about fair taxation, the racial wealth divide, pay equity, responsible wealth, and shareholder activism. Its website contains infographics, videos, and reports on such topics as taxes, income inequality, wealth distribution, and student debt.

Urban Institute
2100 M Street NW
Washington, DC 20037
(202) 833-7200
Website: http://www.urban.org

The Urban Institute is a research institution that seeks to influence public policy by collecting data, evaluating programs, and educating Americans on social and economic issues. Focusing on the problems of cities and urban areas, the Urban Institute offers its research to policy makers, community leaders, and the private sector to diagnose problems and find effective solutions. The organization provides research on a wide variety of topics, such as income and wealth, immigration, tax policies, and employment.

Washington Center for Equitable Growth
1500 K Street NW, 8th Floor
Washington DC 20005
(202) 545-6002

The Washington Center for Equitable Growth is a research and grant-making organization founded to accelerate cutting-edge analysis into whether and how structural changes in the US economy, particularly related to economic inequality, affect economic growth. Its mission is to build a stronger bridge between academics and policy makers so that new research is relevant, accessible, and informative to the policy-making process. Its website provides research, analysis, and data on topics such as credit, minimum wage, employment trends, and income and earnings mobility.

Bibliography of Books

Anthony Atkinson. *Inequality: What Can Be Done?* Cambridge, MA: Harvard University Press, 2015.

Francois Bourguignon. *The Globalization of Inequality*. Princeton, NJ: Princeton University Press, 2015.

Milanovic Branko. *Global Inequality: A New Approach for the Age of Globalization*. Cambridge, MA: Harvard University Press, 2016.

Chuck Collins. *99 to 1: How Wealth Inequality Is Wrecking the World and What We Can Do About It*. San Francisco, CA: Berrett Koehler Publishers, 2012.

Greg. J. Duncan and Richard J. Murnane. *Restoring Opportunity: The Crisis of Inequality and the Challenge for American Education*. Cambridge, MA: Harvard Education Press, 2014.

Harry G. Frankfurt. *On Inequality*. Princeton, NJ: Princeton University Press, 2015.

James K. Galbraith. *Inequality: What Everyone Needs to Know*. New York, NY: Oxford University Press, 2016.

Les Leopold. *Runaway Inequality: An Activist's Guide to Economic Justice*. New York, NY: Labor Institute Press, 2015.

Peter H. Lindert and Jeffrey G. Williamson. *Unequal Gains: American Growth and Inequality since 1700*. Princeton, NJ: Princeton University Press, 2016.

Robert D. Putnam. *Our Kids: The American Dream in Crisis*. New York, NY: Simon & Schuster, 2015.

Tavis Smiley and Cornel West. *The Rich and the Rest of Us: A Poverty Manifesto*. New York, NY: Smiley Books, 2012.

Joseph Stiglitz. *The Great Divide: Unequal Societies and What We Can Do About Them*. New York, NY: W.W. Norton & Company, 2016.

Elizabeth Warren. *A Fighting Chance*. New York, NY: Metropolitan Books, 2014.

Index

A

Alexander, Gary, 65
American Dream, 57–101, 141, 149
  end of, 59–68, 75–81
  where it still exists, 82–96
American Journal of Public Health, 41

B

Babones, Salvatore, 35–40
banking industry, 13, 136, 188
Becker, Gary, 111–114
Birdsong, Nicholas, 173–186
Brandeis, Louis, 151
Brooks, Arthur, 170
Bureau of Labor Statistics, 52, 164
Burke, Allan, 95
Bush, George W., 70

C

capital gains, 37, 38, 40, 135, 142, 143
capitalism, as cause for wealth gap, 187–192
Carlisle, Ashley, 64
Census Bureau, 22, 29–30, 31, 37, 38, 40, 48, 53, 58, 68, 87
Chetty, Raj, 85, 91, 92, 93, 112, 155
child poverty rate, 14, 63, 66, 108
Christiansen, Russ, 89–90
Churchill, Winston, 62
Clinton, Hillary, 166
Coming Apart, 63
"commons," underinvestment in the, 156–157, 160
conservatives, 61–62, 170
Corak, Miles, 69–74
Credit Suisse, 62, 196

crime, increase in because of inequality, 179–180
Current Population Survey (CPS), 164

D

debt, 76, 79, 80, 158
deregulation, 42, 142–143, 154
Desai, Mihir, 160
Dickerson, Mechele, 75–81
Douthat, Ross, 116–117, 118–119
downward mobility as new normal, 75–81

E

education
  benefits for the wealthy, 73–74, 79, 105, 113, 150, 152
  as cause of income inequality, 26, 58, 155, 156
  early, 110, 171, 172
  failure of, 67–68
  free tuition for, 109, 166
  government-provided benefits, 30, 40
  improving/investments in, 33, 105, 120, 126–127, 158, 159, 160
  increased opportunities for lower classes, 168, 171, 172
  level of education and income, 53–54, 73, 84, 185–186
  upward mobility and, 82, 85, 105
Equality of Opportunity Project, 85–86
"Equitable and Sustainable Pensions: Challenges and Experience," 128

F
Federal Reserve, 24, 25, 38, 40, 62, 78, 167
Ferguson, Niall, 59–68
food desert, 181, 183
Fry, Richard, 17, 19–22, 23–27

G
Gallup, 164
Garrett, Thomas A., 18, 28–34
gender earning gap, 155–156
Gini coefficient, 17, 35, 36, 37, 38, 40, 122, 123, 185
   explained, 36–37
Gini, Corrado, 36
globalization, 15, 41, 42, 53–54, 73, 123, 142, 149, 154, 156, 188
Goldin, Claudia, 155–156, 159
government benefits, 35, 38, 39–40, 62, 65–66, 124
Great Depression, 76, 101, 148
Great Divide: Unequal Societies and What We Can Do About Them, The, 58
"Great Gatsby Curve," 69, 70–73, 74, 171
Great Recession of 1980s, 98
Great Recession of 2007–2009, 13, 17, 23, 24, 25, 26, 27, 77, 78, 84, 104, 105, 143, 144, 148, 176, 188
greed, 13, 108, 195

H
Hacker, Jacob, 188
Harvard, 150, 151, 152, 153, 154–156, 158, 160
Hayek, Friedrich, 66
health, decrease in because of inequality, 181–183
health care, 38, 109, 120, 127, 181, 182
Hendren, Nathaniel, 154–155, 157

home ownership, 58, 75, 76–77, 104
household income, 37–38
households, changing composition of American, 52
housing market, 13, 26, 78, 104, 143, 148

I
immigration, 15, 112, 196
income
   defined, 37–38
   difference from wealth, 24, 104
income inequality, 13, 14–15, 17, 164
   arguments that it's not a problem, 28–34, 175–178, 193–197
   partisan divisions on causes of, 26
   perpetuating lower social mobility, 69–74
   reducing, 32–33
   separating from poverty, 46–47
   suggested reasons for, 26, 32–33, 41–44, 45, 52–55, 58
   in United States, 35–40, 114, 132, 170
Income Inequality and the Great Recession, 148
income mobility, 30, 32
infrastructure projects, 106, 108, 143, 156
International Monetary Fund, 120, 121–122, 128

J
Jaynes, Gerald D., 140–145
Jencks, Christopher "Sandy," 154, 158
Jobs, Steve, 193, 194, 197
job training, 33, 54, 127, 160

Johnson, Robert, 91
Joint Economic Committee, 148

K
Katz, Lawrence, 151–152, 155, 158, 159–160
Kochhar, Rakesh, 17, 19–22, 23–27
Krueger, Alan, 65, 70, 71

L
Larino, Jennifer, 193–197
Larson, Spencer, 94–95
layoffs, 13, 24
Lessig, Lawrence, 153–154
Leumer, Bill, 187–192
Lipton, David, 120–128
Lorenz curve, 49–51, 55
lower-income households
    decreasing/stagnating wealth of, 23, 24, 25, 26, 29, 141
    defined, 22, 25

M
Makridis, Christos, 162–167
Mankiw, Greg, 70
Mataconis, Doug, 115–119
McClelland, Edward, 97–101
Medicare, 38, 65, 66, 100, 109, 117, 158
metropolitan areas, loss of middle-income households, 17, 20, 21, 22
middle class/middle-income households
    decreasing/stagnating wealth of, 23, 24, 25, 26, 58, 141, 143, 144, 148, 156
    defined, 22, 25
    median incomes/wealth of, 22, 24
    shrinking of, 17, 19–22, 29, 76, 97–101

minimum wage, 41, 42, 97, 104, 106, 108, 139, 140, 143, 145, 158, 160, 196
Mishel, Lawrence, 168–172
Moving to Opportunity, 155
Murray, Charles, 63
Musk, Elon, 60–61, 68

N
National Public Health Week, 43
"99 percent," 42–44, 113, 192
Northridge, Mary E., 41–44

O
Obama, Barack, 59, 70, 79, 80, 116, 149, 170
Occupy Wall Street movement, 13–14, 17, 36, 41, 42–44, 116, 118, 151
"1 percent, the" 13–14, 15, 17, 32, 42–44, 58, 59, 61, 62, 106, 107, 111, 113, 115, 116, 123, 150, 151, 153, 154, 168, 169–170, 171, 175, 191–192, 196
OpenStax CNX, 45–55
Opposing Viewpoints series, importance of, 10–12
Organisation for Economic Cooperation and Development, (OECD), 38, 40, 67

P
Pathe, Simone, 70
Paycheck Fairness Act, 109
Pazzanese, Christina, 150–161
pensions, 127–128
Peters, Scott, 171
Pew Research Center, 17, 19, 20, 23, 24, 63, 104, 170
Pierson, Paul, 188
Piketty, Thomas, 135
political polarization, 162–167

politics
    income disparity and political
      polarization, 162–167
    wealth and, 152, 153–154, 156,
      178–179, 183–185, 190
"Popular Economics," 194
Posner, Richard, 111–114
poverty, 14, 33, 46–47, 52, 63, 66,
    73, 85, 108, 120, 156, 172, 178,
    185, 186, 191
presidential election of 2016, 14,
    17, 80, 106, 151, 162, 194
Putnam, Robert, 152, 161

Q
quintiles, 17, 29, 30, 31, 54, 55
    measuring income distribution
      by, 47–49

R
redistribution of income/wealth,
    33, 120–128, 143, 171, 178, 186
retirement, 24, 104, 109, 120, 144
    inability to save for, 75, 78–80
Rivkin, Jan, 155, 156–157, 160
Robertson, Ann, 187–192

S
Sachs, Benjamin, 158–159
Sanders, Bernie, 14, 80, 106–110,
    151, 166
Santens, Scott, 129–139
single-parent households, 45, 52,
    63, 65, 73
Skocpol, Theda, 152–153, 159
social mobility, 30, 32, 60, 61, 62,
    63–68, 69–74, 112–114, 116, 152,
    156, 168, 171–172
    downward, 75–81
    upward, 82–96, 111, 115, 149,
      150, 154, 155, 158, 169

Social Security, 38, 39, 65, 66, 100,
    109, 145
Stiglitz, Joseph, 58–59, 188, 189,
    191–192
stock market, 26, 62, 148
subsidies, 31, 93, 124, 188
Summers, Larry, 171

T
Tamny, John, 193, 194–197
taxes/tax policies, 121, 122,
    123–126, 129, 135–136, 154, 158,
    160
    capital gains, 143
    corporations and, 108
    estate taxes, 106
    income taxes, 120, 125, 126,
      140, 142, 145
    indirect, 124
    property taxes, 105
    the wealthy and, 31, 58, 72, 97,
      104, 108, 111–114, 115–119,
      143, 178, 196
Taylor Rule, 167
technology, changes in and
    income, 15, 41, 42, 53–54, 95,
    107, 123, 142, 156, 188
two-earner households, 52
Trump, Donald, 14, 80, 151

U
unemployment rate, 26, 78, 109,
    138, 145, 154, 165–166
unions, 15, 42, 66, 97, 101, 104–
    105, 110, 142, 149, 158–159, 192
United States
    Americans' view of wealth, 195
    Gini coefficient of, 36, 37, 38, 40
    income distribution by quintile,
      47–48
    increase in wealth gap in,
      23–27, 55, 61, 78

ranking in income inequality,
35–40
wealth gap as problem in,
16–55, 148–197
universal basic income (UBI),
129–139
how to pay for, 135–136
improvement to capitalism
with, 133
upper-income households
defined, 22, 25
increase in wealth of, 23, 24, 25,
27, 29, 107–108, 123, 141, 143,
169–170, 196
median wealth of, 24, 25
Urban Institute, 66
US Treasury, 30

V
Vold, Bruce, 83–84, 87, 89, 95–96

W
wages
rise in inequality, 155
shift in distribution of, 52–54
stagnant, 75, 76, 77–78, 85
Wall Street, 107, 108, 110, 151
Warren, Elizabeth, 151
wealth, difference from income,
24, 104
wealth gap
advantages and disadvantages
of, 173–186
being difficult to reverse,
150–161
benefits of reducing, 140–145
government's role in narrowing,
106–110
how it can be addressed,
103–145, 158–161
how it diminishes opportunity,
168–172

impact of in America, 148–197
increase in the, 23–27, 55, 61,
107–108, 121, 128, 170, 175,
177
measuring the, 17
political division and, 162–167
price of inaction, 157–158
as a problem in America,
16–55, 170
"winner take all" labor markets,
47, 52, 53
Wirtz, Ronald A., 82–96
Wolff, Edward, 37, 38, 40, 104

Y
youth job programs, 109